15 short plays for churches

**Chris Chapman, Susan Chapman, Peter Gregory
and Heather Allison**

JBCE

The Joint Board of Christian Education
Melbourne

Published by

THE JOINT BOARD OF CHRISTIAN EDUCATION
Second Floor, 10 Queen Street, Melbourne 3000, Australia

NOAH AND THE TUBES

National Library of Australia
    Cataloguing-in-Publication entry.

Noah and the tubes: 15 short plays for churches

    ISBN: 0 85819 852 5

    1. Christian drama, Australia. 2. Young adult drama, Australian. I. Chapman, Chris, 1957–   .
II. Joint Board of Christian Education.

A822.0516089283

First printed 1992.

Cover illustration by Ben
Cover design by Kelvin Young
Design by Pat Baker
Typeset by JBCE on Ventura Publisher
Printed by Lutheran Publishing House   JB92/3249

Contents

Day 40 The rain has finally stopped Now where did I put that dove?

Ship's Log from the Ark.

Introduction

These plays have been written to be used in a wide variety of situations. Full scale production with costumes, lights and special sound effects is only one option. They are also suitable for readings, quick impromptu sketches, discussion groups and so on. Therefore, a group wishing to stage one or more of the dramas need not be put off by lists of props, stage directions, light and sound effects as, in virtually all cases, easy alternatives are available.

Blackouts and curtains can be replaced by a freeze posture on the last line, followed by a snappy exit to thunderous applause, the inevitable consequence of a fantastic presentation. Obviously, there are many such examples of modifications to staging when the most up to date technology is absent from your performance venue. Equally, it would become tedious for us to list all the alternative possibilities for each play. The best advice is to look at what you have and make your staging arrangements fit those restrictions – simple but effective!

The production of any of these plays comes well within the reach of the average church group with a few chairs, a table, a bottle of glue, two pieces of roughly similar string, the classifieds from any metropolitan newspaper and a bit of imagination (well, perhaps you can forget the classifieds).

Some of the plays contain references to particular people or events that were topical or contemporary at the time of writing. Other names and references may be substituted to make the plays relevant to your situation.

Many characters can be either male or female, depending on the people available to play roles. Just remember to change the 'he', 'she', 'him' and 'her' references where necessary.

Acknowledgments

First and foremost we acknowledge the inspiration of our Lord and Saviour, Jesus Christ, for the endless hours of guidance and tender prompting provided to us for this book. Without that guiding hand these dramas could never have been written. Secondly, we acknowledge that this book would not have been half as much fun to write, and would have taken a third of the time, if it had not been for Eleanor (10 months), Kimberley (22 months) and Rowan (3 3/4) with their wet patches on the floor, feed times and scrunching of scripts. Thank you, kiddies, one and all... NOW GO TO BED!!

NEHEMIAH THE BUILDER

CHARACTERS

Nehemiah	Hasanah
Professor Time-bender	Mrs Hasanah
Servant	Hanun (*a voice*)
Voice over (*may be taped*)	Eliashib (*a voice*)
Dave	Shallum

Several ridiculous voices to shout from offstage. (*Can be anyone offstage at that time.*)

SCENE: *Lights come up on NEHEMIAH working away at a desk on stage right.*

Nehemiah: (*Drunkenly.*) Gidday, I'm Nehemiah (*hic*) and I used to be the king's servant. I used to live in the royal palace in Persia, you know, oh yes I did. I was the royal cup borer... (*tries again*) cup board, core driller, cup bearings, ball bearings, teddy bearings, cup bear... cup... cup... cup carrier. And especially wine taster. It was a good job. You could say I really lapped up my work. But, boy did I get some hangovers. But, seriously now, folks. I'm off it now, I really am. So on with the show. (*Slaps himself in the face and instantly becomes sober and serious.*) Here I am, the real Nehemiah, leader of Israel, as I really was, in my central tent of operations at the walls of Jerusalem.

Servant: (*Rushes excitedly in.*) Sir, sir, the walls are finished. Completed in only ten days, sir ! Jerusalem is safe. Our people are safe ! We've won. The wall is ...

(From offstage there is a terrible, groaning crumbling crash.)

Excuse me, sir. I've just got to go and, er, check on something. (*Hurried exit.*)

Nehemiah: We are having a few problems here with this work crew. You see, very few of them are really builders. Actually, they're only Jewish families – men, women and children – and most know nothing about construction.

Servant: (*Rushes in again.*) Sir. Sir ! It's finished. Really it is this time. In just fifteen days. A total of twenty-five days. We had some difficulties but we didn't let you down, sir. It's all done. There's...

(The familiar rumble and crashes are heard again.)

Well, I'll be off now. Always a little more to do, isn't there? Would you have any sticky tape or string? (*Hurried exit.*)

(Lights blackout. There is a sudden burst of sound as patriotic music briefly plays and then a stirring voice, reminiscent of the old fashioned newsreels, booms out.)

Voice over: Meanwhile, under the blazing merciless sun, our boys are working at the front line against the clock to set heavy bricks in place and construct our first line of defence. Yes, they labour night and day, hour after hour, weapons always at the ready, working with massive blocks and stones, moving them piece by piece, one by one, until they stretch away into the distance to form...

(The familiar rumbles and crashes are heard again.)

... sort of a big pile of rubble.

(Lights come up again.)

Nehemiah: What happened this time?

Servant: Well, sir. You live and learn. It's one of those little mistakes that anyone could have made. But we won't make it next time. Oh, no sir. Next time we *will* remember to cement the bricks together, and believe me, when I find out whose fault it is... well, I've got to be going now, sir. I have an important phone call coming. *(Hurried exit.)*

Nehemiah: Why me? Why me??

(Knock, knock.)

Yes ?

Dave: *(Enters. He is dressed in builders attire, for example blue singlet and stubbies with a hammer belt. A roll of plans is in his hand. He has a drawling Australian accent, very confident and oblivious to his incompetence.)*

Excuse me.

Nehemiah: What is it ?

Dave: You tryna build a wall or something?

Nehemiah: Yes, what of it?

Dave: Well you got big problems, mate. You want help from me Dave and me Dad? We can build this wall for you quick cause we are the Dave and Dad Homes and Walls Construction Company. Nice quick work on all our jobs and some of them are still standing.

Nehemiah: No, really. I think we'll be alright.

Dave: No problems, matey. This nice man called Sanballet, he told me, Dave my boy, you go and help those Jewish types build their wall and here I am. *(Spreads plans out.)* Now I got the plans right here. You can see we put the wall up in three days, bog it up good in all the cracks. Nice plaster job and painting thrown in free. Waterproof section for the wailing wall and guarantee for lifetime unless it falls down in which case we'll deny we ever saw it and you won't be able to phone us cause we'll be out of the country. Just sign here, please.

Nehemiah: I don't think we need any help, thanks !

Dave: But you don't know what you're missing, mate. We do it all for you nice and easy. We do a lot of this work, like that other wall we built. Where was that? Ah yes. Jericho. Now that was one heck of a good wall. It will make us famous one day. Really something to blow your trumpet about. You'd just fall for it.

Nehemiah: Out!

Dave: You don't like my plans?

Nehemiah:	I don't like your puns. Out!!
Dave:	Okay, but you'll be sorry. We'll see the union about this. *(Starts offstage calling as he goes.)* Okay, Dad, warm up the truck. We'll take that shipbuilding job on the Titanic after all.
Servant:	*(Rushes in, holding a saw with the teeth upwards and is pointing to the smooth side.)* Just a quick question, sir. It's this side of the saw on the wood isn't it? *(Sees the murderous look in Nehemiah's eyes and races out again.)*
Nehemiah:	*(Close to cracking.)* It's all getting too much for me. Everyone wants to help but nobody knows anything about building. Ever since I was a cupbearer, and I heard about the plight of the Jews here, I have been driven by a vision, a goal, to build these walls. *(He is becoming melodramatic.)* Deep in the dark, subconscious regions of my mind, I hear the voices urging me on.

(Several ridiculous voices, cracked and quavering shout from offstage, 'Go on! Go on!')

(Gasp!) There they are. Like an angel choir. But we aren't getting anywhere. I need help, Lord. An angel descending from above in a fiery chariot burning with the knowledge of how to rebuild the wall in fifty-two days. Send him now!

(PROFESSOR TIME-BENDER enters to theme music.)

Professor Time-bender:	Hi!!, I'm Professor Time-bender, bender, bender, time traveller. Together with my faithful companion what's her name, I traverse the bounds of time and space in a Westinghouse refrigerator carton in search of truth, rust and Neville the deranged robot.

(The emphasis on Professor Time-bender's name is meant to emulate an echo and is produced by the actor, not electronically.)

Nehemiah:	What about the fiery chariot, Lord.
Servant:	*(Rushing in.)* Sir, sir. The people need encouragement. You must go out and speak to them. Here they are, building the walls of their city, their homeland, their faith. Their minds are filled with religious and nationalistic fervour. Their hearts beat proud. Their veins run hot with the blood of... what nationality did you say we were, sir?
Nehemiah:	Aghhh!!

(SERVANT exits.)

It's hopeless. Hopeless!

Professor Time-bender:	Are you a little upset about something?
Nehemiah:	These walls are driving me nuts!
Professor Time-bender:	Driving you up the wall, eh?
Nehemiah:	*(Sob.)*
Professor Time-bender:	What seems to be the problem?
Nehemiah:	We've got to build them as fast as we can or our enemies will wipe us out. But no one knows much about building and I've got to co-ordinate it all.

7

Professor Time-bender: Well, let's go and take a look at the problem on site.

Nehemiah: Do you really think that would help?

Professor Time-bender: Well it can't hurt, can it?

> *(At this point, lights can blackout if you wish to change set, shift things, etc. A voice offstage can say something intelligent like: 'Stay tuned for the next exciting episode to this exciting drama. But in the meantime, this ancient Bechuanaland proverb will help you on your way through life. [A tongue-twisting blather of savage grunts and made up language follows.] And don't ever forget it. And now, back to the walls of Jerusalem.' Lights then come up again. NEHEMIAH and the PROFESSOR TIME-BENDER enter walking along talking and inspecting imaginary walls.)*

Nehemiah: *(Looking towards downstage as if the walls are along the front of the audience section.)* Look at this!

Professor Time-bender: What's wrong with it?

Nehemiah: Well, look. They've painted the walls green. With flower boxes and petunias. Who ever heard of a defensive wall that looked like that?! Who's doing this section?

Professor Time-bender: *(Looking at the plans in his hand.)* It says, Shallum and his daughters, for Better Homes and Gardens.

Nehemiah: Landscape gardeners. I might have known. Shallum!!

Shallum: *(Runs onto stage.)* Hi, are you admiring the wall? It's got a great ambience, hasn't it? Really organic.

Nehemiah: Get this wall bricked up NOW!

Professor Time-bender: And make it solid.

Shallum: Oh alright. Some people have no artistic sense whatever.

> *(They walk on a little. The sound of sheep bleating is heard over the sound system.)*

Professor Time-bender: What's that sound?

Nehemiah: Sounds like sheep to me. What section are we up to?

Professor Time-bender: *(Reading plans.)* The Sheep Gate.

Nehemiah: *(Stopping dead and pointing.)* Oh no! Look at it! Who's in charge here?

Professor Time-bender: It says, the priests, led by Eliashib.

Nehemiah: Eliashib! Where are you?

Eliashib: What do you want?

Nehemiah: What's this supposed to be?

Eliashib: The Sheep Gate. We promised we'd rebuild it. Don't you like it?

Professor Time-bender: *(Doubtfully.)* Oh, it's very nice.

Nehemiah: But it's not exactly what we wanted.

Eliashib: Why? What's wrong with it?

Professor Time-bender: Well... it's made out of sheep.

Eliashib: Well it *is* the Sheep Gate. What did you expect?

Nehemiah: But you can't mount a defensive city wall gate by rivetting sheep to hinges and having them swinging about to open and shut.

Professor Time-bender: We need doors and gates of solid timber.

Eliashib: Oh, well, then it would be a timber gate wouldn't it?

Nehemiah: Look. Sheep Gate is just a name! Make it out of timber!

Eliashib: Well, I'll tell you what. We'll put on timber doors and install bolts and bars as long as we can still nail a few sheep on too. Just a couple.

Nehemiah: Well, alright. *(To the Professor.)* What's next?

Professor Time-bender: You aren't going to like it.

Nehemiah: What is it?

Professor Time-bender: The Manure Gate.

Nehemiah: Oh, well then, we'll give it a miss.

Professor Time-bender: At least you can be sure no one will attack you from there.

Nehemiah: The laundromat in the area must be doing a good trade.

(They walk on some more.)

Professor Time-bender: Right. This is getting interesting. Next we come to... a big, er, hole in the wall.

Nehemiah: Now what's this supposed to be?

Professor Time-bender: *(Referring to plans.)* It's marked, the Valley Gate. Hanun is in charge here.

Nehemiah: Hanun! Hanun! Where are you?

Professor Time-bender: *(Strains eyes in distance.)* Hey, who's that down there, in the valley?

Nehemiah: *(Looking too.)* It's Hanun. And he's building a gate. Hanun! What's that?

Hanun: *(Very distant but still audible.)* The Valley Gate.

Nehemiah: You great lump! What's the use of a gate down there? You can go round either side of it. It won't protect anyone!

Hanun: Oh, yeah. Well do you want us to build a wall on either side too?

Nehemiah: No, fool. We've got a wall half-built up here!

Hanun: Well, do you want us to shift the wall down here?

Professor Time-bender: Bring the gate up here.

Hanun: Okay. Do you want us to bring the valley too?

Nehemiah: No! *(To Professor.)* Well, we seem to be sorting a few things out round here.

Servant: *(Rushes on.)* Sir, sir. There are three fierce men at the main gate, Sanballet, Gesham and Tobiah. They say they'll get the Builders Union to call a strike on your work site if you don't employ Dave and Dad.

Nehemiah: Tell them to nick off. We can look after ourselves.

Servant: Right. *(Exits.)*

Professor Time-bender: Along we go to the next gate and there we have... oh, look.

> *(He has seen HASANAH and MRS HASANAH who have entered and are standing, weeping.)*

Nehemiah: Wonder what's wrong with them.

Professor Time-bender: Excuse me. What's the matter? Who are you, anyway?

Hasanah: *(Sobbing.)* I'm Hasanah.

Mrs Hasanah: *(Sobbing.)* And I'm Mrs Hasanah.

Hasanah: And we're weeping.

> *(They sob and rave again. Professor and NEHEMIAH are somewhat nonplussed by this startling piece of information.)*

Professor Time-bender: But why?

Hasanah: Because we're in debt.

Professor Time-bender: No you're not. You're in Jerusalem.

Mrs Hasanah: No, in debt. We owe.

Professor Time-bender: Oh.

Mrs Hasanah: No need to repeat it.

Hasanah: We had to sell the children to pay off our debts.

Professor Time-bender: What?

Nehemiah: You sold your own children?

Mrs Hasanah: Yes, for two shekels.

Hasanah: Two shekels for our children.

Nehemiah: Shocking.

Hasanah: Yes. Their education cost us five shekels.

Mrs Hasanah: We made a sixty percent loss!

> *(They fall to even more exaggerated weeping.)*

Professor Time-bender: Something has to be done about this situation.

Nehemiah: You're right. I'll take it to court, that's what I'll do. Look, it's been nice meeting you but I'd better go now. I can view the rest of this wall tomorrow, but I'll have to see the priests about this debt thing. Thanks for your help. Bye. *(To the HASANAHs.)* Right, you two. Off we go. *(They exit.)*

Professor Time-bender: *(Melodramatically.)* There he goes. Nehemiah. Once again the great leader and inspirer of his people. He didn't give up. He never threw in the towel. *(To audience.)* And you, too, as you go on through life and build your own walls and construct your own gates, you too, will come across the Daves, the Dads, the Sanballets, Geshams and Tobiahs. People who try to lead you from the right path. Why say, 'Come on, do it the easy way'. Be like Nehemiah. Go down your God-given path and never give up. *(Solemnly.)* And now, I go. Forge on ahead. Never give up. Remember what I said. Goodbye.

(He crosses and climbs into his time machine. There is the sound of a car engine turning over weakly. It goes again and again. Professor's voice is heard getting more and more frustrated.)

Professor Time-bender: Start. Come on, start!

(He climbs out again and begins to jump up and down, ranting and kicking at the machine, finally dragging it off.)

Professor Time-bender: You won't start will you? You rotten pile of scrap metal. I give up on you. I've had it with you. Start! START!! I hate you, etc...

(Lights go down as he exits. PROFESSOR TIME-BENDER theme music may play.)

Nehemiah wanted everyone to help with the building of the new walls, but he had no idea how this new guy in the armour and with one arm could help.

QUESTIONS FOR DISCUSSION

It would be helpful to learn something of the background to the Jewish exile in Babylon (2 Kings 24 and 25, and 2 Chronicles 36). An explanation should also be provided of the position of Nehemiah as cupbearer (Nehemiah 2:1-3), and the way this position brought Nehemiah into close contact with the King.

1. If Nehemiah was living so prosperously in Susa (Persia), why should he feel so concerned about what was happening in Jerusalem (Nehemiah Chapter 1)?

2. When faced with challenge or danger, Nehemiah characteristically reacted in two ways (1:10-11; 4:8-9; 4:14). Describe these and discuss whether they are still relevant to you, and in what situations.

3. Have a look at the lists of workers in Chapter 3. Note particularly 3:1, 3:12 and 3:13. What problems would be encountered with such a work crew? Why, in spite of these problems, were they successful?

4. Note 3:23. Why do you think people were put in charge of sections of the wall that were closest to their own homes?

5. Describe the reaction of other local tribes (4:1-9; 6:1-7; 2:19) Why do you think they reacted in this way?

6. What can we learn about the response of Nehemiah and his people? (4:10-13 and 16-23)

7. Even in such a situation where cooperation and solidarity was called for, there were still opportunists. See 5:1-5 and compare to Exodus 22:25. Why do you think these people acted in such a way?

8. Are there parallels of this sort of behaviour in our own world which is under threat from overpopulation, nuclear pollution and environmental chaos?

ADAM AND EVE

CHARACTERS:

Voice over 1	Eve
Voice over 2	God
Adam	Person

SCENE: *Music plays 'You must remember this'*

Voice over 1: Scene one, repossession warehouse for used Old Testament characters. Do you ever wonder what happens to all those Old Testament characters that you hear about for a while then forget? When their time is up, they get put into one of these warehouses where they can be re-cycled whenever necessary. What do they do there? Well, they relax, they sit around and remember the old days, they think, they recall, they... *(sings)*... go walking in the dark, dancing in the park and reminiscing.

Voice over 2: Stop that singing.

Voice over 1: But I want to.

Voice over 2: I tell you to stop singing.

Voice over 1: No. *(sings)* Walking in the park, dancing in the... *(pistol shot)* ... *(speaking)* Oh alright. And now two of our original favourites, Adam and Eve.

(ADAM and EVE enter, dressed in old fashioned but grand attire.)

Adam: You must remember this, a kiss is just a kiss... Ah Eve, my lovely Eve, first woman of all creation, loveliest of all God's creations, Eve baby.

Eve: Yes, dear. *(EVE bats her eyelids at ADAM.)*

Adam: *(To audience)* Sometimes I wonder whether it was worth the rib. *(Speaks to Eve)* Think back, baby, to what it used to be, back in the garden, just you and me, the trees around, a glass of wine, a Paris cafe...

Eve: Slight exaggeration, dear.

Adam: Yes, perhaps, but remember how it used to be, all those years ago, millions of ages back, in the prehistoric ages of the primitive earth, when the universe was young?

Eve: Yes, dear, even *(name of prominent person)* wasn't around then.

Adam: Do you remember those ancient days before the flood, when strange creatures roamed the earth? Yes, they are all extinct now, except for a few remaining freaks, like lungfish, platypus and *(name of prominent person)*. Let's look back in our minds.

Eve: I can't see anything.

Adam: Let's think back to the old days. Remember when we first met? You were just standing there, and I had been...

(Lights fade to blackout.)

Voice over 1: Bearing in mind that the following scene concerns the earliest days of Adam and Eve, the board of censors has determined that the standards of clothing might be offensive to most people, and therefore the stage will remain darkened. How do I know it's offensive? Well I've been to see it five times, and believe me it is. And so the stage will be dark, except that I have a torch here, and... hey, give me that torch, come on, it's mine... The anti-discrimination board has subsequently determined that the performance cannot be altered in any way, and so respectfully asks that audience members use their imagination in order to clothe the actors.

(Lights up on ADAM, fully clothed, in rustic 'garden-wear'.)

Voice over 2: Hey, great imagining!

God: Adam, I give you this garden as your home. In it, I have created everything to satisfy your needs.

Adam: OOOOh thank you.

God: I give you the trees, tall, magnificent and strong, for shelter and beauty.

Adam: Oh yes lovely.

God: I give you the bubbling streams of water to slake your thirst.

Adam: Mmm, nice.

God: I give you the fruits of the fields and trees for food.

Adam: Thanks, that'll be great.

God: I give you the animals for your company, use and service.

Adam: Thanks.

God: And last, but certainly not least...

Adam: Yes?

God: My very finest creation...

Adam: Yes? Yes?

God: I give you woman.

Adam: What? Oh, alright. Well thanks for everything, God, we'll be going now.

God: Wait a moment.

Adam and Eve: Huh?

God: These are a few things you have to do.

Adam and Eve: Huh?

God: A few responsibilities.

Adam and Eve: Responsibilities?

God: Adam, you must tend and care for this garden.

Adam: What, all this? And you didn't even give me a mower.

God: And Eve, you must help and support Adam in his work, and care for him and he for you.

Eve:	What, all the time?
God:	And, Adam, you must give names to the fruits and beasts of the field.
Adam:	What? All of them? How am I supposed to do that?
God:	Well it's quite simple. There, pick up that piece of fruit and name it.
Adam:	Ummmmm. Peach.
God:	What made you call it that?
Adam:	Well it's written on the box, isn't it? Oh come on, I can't look after all of this, couldn't someone else do it?
Eve:	Yes, I don't want this responsibility stuff because it sounds like hard work to me. I want to complain.
Adam:	Yes, you complain, dear. You know what they say about the squeaky wheel getting the grease.
Eve:	The squeaky what?
Adam:	Never mind.
Eve:	Lord, couldn't you turn one of the lions into a butler or something, then we could sit around and give him orders.
God:	Listen, I gave you this garden as a gift of love. The least you could do is to look after it and love it and love me.
Eve:	Couldn't we change it for a modular home and a permanently full fridge?
Adam:	Full of food and drinks and fruit too?
Eve:	You know what they say, an apple a day keeps... Oh, I have a feeling I shouldn't have said that.
God:	The responsibility is yours, and furthermore, you must not eat of the fruit of the tree of knowledge or all will be ruined.
Adam:	What, all these rules too?
Eve:	We'll start a union, that's what we'll do.
Adam:	And we'll have rolling strikes, but only on grassy areas.
God:	I can see I'm going to have trouble with these two.
	(Lights fade and rise again on ADAM and EVE in original gear.)
Adam:	*(Humming refrain of song.)* Ah yes, hardly seems like yesterday. But now, we're out of the garden and into the big bad world and all because you could not follow a simple rule.
Eve:	What???
Adam:	Well you ate it.
Eve:	The snake told me to.
Adam:	I never saw any snake, just you feeding your face with fruit.
Eve:	Don't try to put the blame on me, mate.
Adam:	No, no, of course not, dear.

(If necessary, the drama can be split into two episodes at this point. If two episodes are required, include the following voice over lines. If one episode is required, resume script at next ADAM line.)

Voice over 1: *(ADAM and EVE freeze.)* Can this be the end for Adam and Eve? Will they ever eat apples again? And just how will they resolve the tricky question of who is to blame for original sin? Find out as they continue their trip down memory lane in the next exciting episode of *(sings)* reminiscing. *(Sound of gunshot.)*

(End of first episode)

Voice over 1: And now we return you to Adam and Eve who are just sitting around, remembering, recalling and... *(begins to sing)* walking in the... *(sound of gunshot)*

Voice over 2: I thought I warned you about that song.

Adam: Eve baby, think back now, you must remember this, a kiss is just a kiss, think back to the old days.

Eve: Yes, they were lovely people, old Mrs Day was such a sweetie.

Adam: Not the people, the time! Remember, when we had just been thrown out of the garden, into the outer world?

Eve: Yes, dear, it was awful, nowhere to go, cold and lonely.

(Lights fade and rise again on ADAM and EVE in garden gear, with suitcases. They approach a person behind a desk, or the following scene could be played with ADAM using a telephone and using a voice over.)

Person: Morning, Housing Commission, Can I help you?

Adam: Hello, I... *(EVE stands on his toe or similar)* ... We want a house.

Person: Yes, what name, please?

Adam: Adam and Eve.

Person: Surname?

Adam: ... er... *(Looks puzzled)*

Person: Yes and where was your last place of residence?

Adam: Garden of Eden.

Person: *(Laughs, disbelieving)* Oh yes, north or south side.

Adam: Listen you, we are Adam and Eve, the originals, and we need a place to live.

Person: Oh, that Adam and Eve.

Adam: Yes, that Adam and Eve.

Person: Oh yes, I've heard all about you two. Wasn't it you who messed up the garden?

Eve: Oh no, that wasn't us, that was a different Adam and Eve.

Adam: It was our twin brother and sister. Er, we do need a house.

Person: Well, you'll have to look after it and keep it clean, and there'll be a yard.

Adam and Eve: We'll do it, we'll do it.

Person: Well you never lived up to your responsibility in the garden. God wasn't very happy with that episode, you know.

Adam: But we didn't mean...

Person: And in any case, we haven't any houses on file, I'm afraid. We're booked out expecting a big rush when Moses leads the children of Israel out of Egypt.

Eve: Oh.

Adam: Could you just look?

Person: There's no point, we don't have a single house.

Adam: None?

Person: Not one. *(Browses through book)*... Wait on, Adam and Eve, wasn't it?

Adam and Eve: Yes??

Person: Well, there's a house booked in your name here.

Eve: Us?? But who would book a house for us?

Adam: Yes, who booked it for us?

Person: God.

Adam and Eve: God??

Eve: Maybe God doesn't hate us. Maybe God still loves us after all.

Adam: Yeah, even if we can't go back to the garden.

Eve: God's still looking out for us.

Adam: And always will!

(Curtain. Fade lights.)

QUESTIONS FOR DISCUSSION

1. Read Genesis 1:26-31. What responsibilities did God give to the newly created people? See also Genesis 2:15-19.

2. What special provisions did God make for them?

3. What relationship is there, at that stage of the story, between humans and animals, plants and the physical world?

4. Read Genesis 3:1-5. What arguments are used to persuade the woman to eat the fruit?

5. How did the humans try to avoid the responsibility for their actions? (Read Genesis 3:8 and 3:10-12.)

6. In what ways is the universe structured to make us responsible for the consequences of our actions?

7. How much should people take the blame for the current state of the world, in terms of politics, environment, economy, war, poverty, overpopulation, etc? (Galatians 6:7-8 and Job 4:8 may help your discussion.)

PROFESSOR TIME-BENDER AND THE RUNNING OF THE GREAT TEMPTATION OBSTACLE COURSE

(Episode One)

CHARACTERS:

James
John
St Peter
Professor Time-bender
Mother of James and John

Voice over narrator
Negro singer *(voice over)*
Matron Scum
German accented voice over

SCENE:	*Curtains closed. Voice over with humming of negro spiritual in the background.*
Voice over:	*(From backstage)* Years ago deep in the American south, amid the cotton fields and plantations, the negro spiritual was born. This was a deeply melodic form of music, it gave voice to the woes, the hopes, and the beliefs of the negro slaves. Images of heaven were frequently used and the most common of these was that of the pearly gates.
Negro singer:	Pearly gates am pearly white all shinin' in de light.
	Gonna cross dat Jordan chilly and cold *(Brrrr.)*
	Gonna go where tings is right.
	Swing low
	(Tarzan background.)
	Sweet chariot,
	Take me to dem pearly gates.
	Brudders, sisters, aunties uncles cousins,
	Take me to dem pearly gates.
	Oh yeah, dem pearly gates.
	(Spoken)
	They're sort of a translucent white and richly carved in a neo-Georgian style reminiscent of Bramante's Florentine Cathedral doors and can I stop talking like this now?
Voice over:	Scene one. De pearly gates.
	(Curtain opens. JAMES and JOHN rush on screaming and pushing. Stop mid stage.)
James:	Wait, wait. Stop. Let's approach this like rational adults.
John:	Right.
James:	Look over there.
John:	Where?

(JAMES pushes him out of the way.)

James:	Ha ha beat you there.
Mum:	Get a move on. Stop your fighting.

(She strides on.)

John:	It's not fair what he did. I wanted to be first to the door.
Mum:	Ah stop your whinging.
James:	What do we do now, mum?
Mum:	Ring the bell, of course!
John:	Huh?
Mum:	Do I have to do everything?
James:	But, mum, it's the pearly gates. Do you think we should?
Mum:	Look, ring that bell or I'll give you what for. You want to be top one day, don't you?
John:	Yeah but...
Mum:	I'm gonna lose my temper in a minute and you know what that means.
James:	Aw mum, you wouldn't.
Mum:	I will. There'll be no *(Insert the name of a popular T.V. show)* for a week.
James:	I'll ring it.
John:	No you won't, I'll ring it.
James:	It's all mine. I got here first.

(Characters ad lib a brawl. MUM raises her eyes to heaven, then stamps over and stands over them. By now they are on their knees at each others throats. She grabs a head in each hand and belts them together.)

Mum:	Ring it together at the same time.

(They do so.)

Receptionist's voice:	Pearly gates reception service. This is a recorded message. The pearly gates will be open for new comers between the hours of 9 and 5. Visitors are welcome from 12 till 3. If an emergency arises, hit the gong and call for Peter. Thank you.
James:	Hit the gong, quick.

(JOHN does so.)

John:	Must be no one home.
Mum:	That's not loud enough.

(Belts his head. The sound effect of a cymbal crashing is heard.)

St Peter:	If that's the Cravon lady, go way and take your rotten dark rinse with you. It only turned my hair green.
John:	Peter, come out here. It's me, John.

St Peter:	No thanks, I've already got one.
James:	No it's us, James and John, your old mates. Come out quick, we've gotta see you.
St Peter:	How do I know it's you. Did you bring some identification or distinguishing mark by which I may identify you ?
Mum:	Stop your nonsense, Peter, and get out here. I'll give you a hiding if you don't.
St Peter:	Ah your mother. Yes, I remember her. I'll be right out.
	(PETER comes out.)
Mum:	It's about time too. I've been standing out here half the day knocking and ringing, waiting to get my boys an audience. What type of service is this anyway? Now I'm not moving from this spot until I...
St Peter:	Hello, Tony! *(or similar current game show host)*
Mum:	Tony who?
St Peter:	Tony. You know, that good looking fellow on the T.V. Looks like him anyway.
Mum:	Tony!!! Oh, how wonderful. You boys know what to do. Get going. *(She races off after the imaginary 'Tony'.)* Yoo hoo. Tonyyyy! I watched you on 'Sale of the Millenium' last night and you were just wonderful. The way you...
St Peter:	Hee hee. Wonder who it really was. Now what's this all about? Come on, hurry up, I've got to get back and see the rest of episode 488879 of Days of our Eternal Lives.
John:	I've got to get into the kingdom of God.
St Peter:	Why?
John:	Because I want to be number one, that's why.
James:	Ah, you'll be number one clown in the celestial circus, that's about all. I'm gonna be number one, so let me through them pearly gates, quick.
John:	Ah, you great Samaritan. What would you know?
	(They brawl again.)
St Peter:	Quiet, quiet, quiet!!!
John:	I'll do anything to get in first.
James:	I'm better than him. I've been training for months.
St Peter:	Be quiet.
John:	Anyway, I sat on his right hand when he was on earth with us.
James:	Yeah, sat on his right hand and nearly broke all his fingers too.
John:	Only because I couldn't get near him because you were always in the way. Anyway I wrote more chapters in the Bible than you did.

James: Yeah, well my chapters are better. I'll win this competition to get in here if it's the last...

St Peter: Quiet! What's all this about competing to get in?

John: I'm ready for any task. Tell me what I have to do to get into the kingdom of God. I'll beat him to it no trouble and get myself in...

St Peter: But...

James: Come on, tell us. Don't hide anything. What do you want me to do? Run 100 miles? I'll do it.

John: Weight lifting?

James: Battling monsters?

John: Discus?

James: Javelin?

John: Bingo?

St Peter: So you want to compete do you? Well I ought to tell you...

(JAMES and JOHN ad lib screams about wanting to compete.)

Well, I guess we can arrange something.

(Cheers. The sound of a bell is heard and the characters look around, wondering what is happening.)

German accented voice over: Let's just pause a moment to think. *(ding)* Let's go back to *(ding)* oooh, excuse me. *(ding)* Ooh, I'll never eat Mexican food again. It really comes back to haunt you. It's the celestial psychologist here, Dr Angelbrain, the heavenly headshrinker. I'd like to pause a moment to analyse the overdeveloped achievement motivation of these boys. *(ding)* Ooh, the hot ones really burn. Let's hear what the lady in charge of the divine nursery has to say about the behaviour of these lads even before they were born. Here is Matron Scum.

(Old woman in a nurses uniform shuffles on stage and sees the boys.)

Matron Scum: Oh James and John, I remember them.

James: Hey look, it's the matron.

John: She used to love us.

Matron Scum: I was always separating them, the little brats. They were always fighting so much about who was the best. Bad tempered little beggars too. Called down fire and brimstone on me once and nearly burned all the hairs off me legs.

German accented voice over: And thank you, matron. I hope that brings some sanity and sense to the episode. Now it's back to the shock treatment unit for you. I'll cure Saul's depression if it's the last thing I do.

St Peter: Well if you fellows are so intent on competing...

James: Look, Peter old mate. Just a tiny peek through the gates, fifty dollars. I'll come back, I promise.

John: Look at that, Peter. This is the type of man you are dealing with, who would bribe you for fifty dollars. I'll give you sixty.

St Peter: I'll forget you said that. Now for a competition we'll need an adjudicator. Someone who's fair, objective, with a keen sense of the athletic. Someone who really knows quality when he sees it, a super being who shall descend from above. Who shall it be?

(PROFESSOR TIME-BENDER theme music plays as he enters on his 'spaceship'.)

Professor Time-bender: Okay, my little rose petal, this is it... Surfers Paradise. Excuse me, can you direct me to the Chevron? *(or similar holiday resort)*

St Peter: The what?

Professor Time-bender: You mean this isn't Surfers Paradise?

St Peter: This is everybody's paradise, matey.

Professor Time-bender: Drat, missed it by seven letters. Well anyway it's close.

(Back inside)

Okay, my little dove, put the bikinis away and get out the coffee pot. You're not mad at me are you, dear?

(Sound effect of a hollow bong. PROFESSOR TIME-BENDER emerges again with saucepan jammed down over his head.)

St Peter: Will you be our judge?

Professor Time-bender: No, I don't bear a grudge.

St Peter: No, our judge.

Professor Time-bender: No thank you, I don't like fudge.

James: Take the saucepan off your head, you can't hear.

Professor Time-bender: Hold on I'll take the saucepan off my head, I can't hear.

John: The guy's not functioning at all well.

Professor Time-bender: Watch it boy, I heard that.

St Peter: What in the world are you?

Professor Time-bender: I'm Professor Time-bender, bender, bender, bender, time traveller. Together with my faithful companion what's her name, I traverse time and space in a Westinghouse refrigerator carton, in a never ending search for truth, rust and Neville the deranged robot.

(The emphasis on Professor Time-bender's name is meant to emulate an echo and is produced by the actor, not electronically.)

St Peter: That's all very nice but we need a judge and since you are here, you're it, boy.

Professor Time-bender: What for?

John: I'm gonna be first in the kingdom of God.

James: I am, you don't stand a hope.

Professor Time-bender: I get the picture.

St Peter: We'll give them the great temptation obstacle course. That'll make them happy.

(Cheers from JAMES and JOHN.)

St Peter: Now I want fair play at all times. Here are the rules. *(Flashes a sheet of paper in front of their eyes.)*... any questions?

James and John: No, no.

St Peter: Right, then, if you want to compete... compete. *(Points off left. JAMES and JOHN rush off in that direction cheering.)*

Professor Time-bender: Which way is the obstacle course by the way? *(PETER points off right.)*

St Peter: Who says I don't have a sense of humour? The other way only leads to the...

(Screams fading from off.)

Oh well, they can say hello to Judas while they're down there.

(Blackout.)

Voice over: Well, that ends the first exciting episode of...

Negro singer: Swing low

Voice over: Be quiet.

Negro singer: Sorry.

(Episode Two)

SCENE: *Sports music as curtain rises to reveal PROFESSOR TIME-BENDER at table with binoculars.*

Professor Time-bender: Well, here we are at the Great Temptation Obstacle Course for the running of the Great Temptation Race for the first time since those forty days in the wilderness when the competitor got through every one. Today we have James and John, two very confident lads competing for first place in the kingdom of Heaven. Live commentary provided by you know who. It's a fine day and we have a capacity crowd of all the well knowns here today. I can see Solomon over there with his nine hundred wives and he's sitting in his gold plated, er, wheel chair. Daniel's over there feeding glue to some lions. Mary and Martha have a Devonshire tea stall by the outer stand and I can see someone digging up the pitch, it's probably the lazy servant of Matthew 25 looking for his lost talent. Mary Magdalene is running a shoe shine there buffing up shoes with her hair and free Dixieland Jazz is being provided by General Joshua and the Wallbreaker Trumpet Ensemble. Also er...

(Hand comes up from beneath table and grabs his microphone. MUM appears.)

Mum: Hello, all you wonderful people out there in temporal television land. This is coming to you live via celestial satellite and I'm here to see my boys do their stuff and pass their tests. I trained 'em for this, you know, and my boys are gonna be number one in the...

Professor Time-bender: Give me that mike. Well, it's the first event of the afternoon, the crossing of the balance beam suspended over the Valley of the Shadow of Death. They're limbering up and... they seem to have started... and oh dear, John has tackled James from behind and James has kicked him. Now they're wrestling on the beam, they're strangling each other, there's punches flying...

Mum: Keep your balance, you idiots...

(Sound effect of screams fading to silence.)

I told them not to fight, didn't I, but they wouldn't listen would they, oh no... what are you looking at?

Professor Time-bender: Is that Tony over there again?

Mum: Tony!!

Professor Time-bender: Or is it Sir Reginald Very Rich-Person?

Mum: Sir Reginald!! Don't go way. Yoo hoo. It's me again. *(Races off.)*

Professor Time-bender: Well, the heli-angel surf rescue squad has just winched the boys out of the Valley and they're ready for their next attempt which is the high jump over the hedge of pride and the mud patch of the fall. They're loosening up now and... and there they go. They've taken their jumps and it looks good but oh no, John has grabbed James by the hair and is squirting a can of cola up his nose. James is ripping out the hairs on John's legs. They're fighting in mid air. They're going to land in the...

(Sound effect of falling into mud.)

Well, it just goes to show that pride goeth before a *(raspberry)*. And now it's onto the next event which is the perilous swim through the custard of gluttony avoiding the prunes of sloth. The boys are on the diving blocks now and *(raspberry)* John's in and *(raspberry)* James is in and they're swimming. John is making no progress at all mainly because James has tied his feet to the block. Meanwhile, James is noticing the millstone John tied round his neck. While they bale out the pool to try and find him, we'll tally up the scores. John nil. James nil. Well, it doesn't look as if either of them is doing too well at getting himself into the kingdom of Heaven. Now for the final event we have the distance run of patience and endurance. This is a tense moment in the games because it could provide the deciding points for one or the other. All quiet for the start please.

(Sound effect of a female giggling.)

Oh come on, Solomon, stop it now, eh? There they go into the straight and John is still picking himself out of the dirt because James has stapled his soles to the track, but I think that any time now...

(Sound effect explosion.)

Yes, there go the bombs John put into James' socks. John is off down the track to catch him. James is flying through the air. John is catching up. Oh no, James has landed on top of him and they've knocked each other out cold. I can see their mum out there fanning them and giving them copious amounts of vitamin 'pick me ups', but time is ticking away. They're staggering off into the home straight now, but I'm afraid it's all over. Time is long gone as they come in, two very tired lads.

(JAMES ands JOHN covered in dirt and muck stagger on stage with mum poking them along. Both put their arms up for victory.)

Professor Time-bender: That brings the scores to a grand total of... nil all. You both flunked.

(They both deflate.)

James: I flunked better than you did.

John: You did not. I flunked the best.

(They are arguing away centre stage when a person walks across stage to the pearly gates, speaks shortly to PETER and goes inside.)

John: Hey, how come he got in?

James: He didn't have to do anything. Look at all we had to go through.

St Peter: What do you mean all you *had* to go through. You didn't *have* to go through anything.

James and John: WHAT??

St Peter: You don't have to compete to get in here. That's what I tried to tell you before, but you were so intent on beating each other you wouldn't listen.

John: But but, all the, but... Wahhhhh!

James: What do we have to do, then?

St Peter: You have to answer a question truthfully.

Mum: What's the question? They've both studied very hard for this.

John: I studied harder than you did.

(They ad lib their argument which is broken up by PETER, PROFESSOR TIME-BENDER and MUM.)

St Peter: The question is... have you accepted Jesus Christ as your personal Lord and saviour?

Both: Yes.

St Peter: Welcome.

John: You mean that's all?

St Peter: Of course that's all. You didn't think you could work your way into the kingdom of Heaven, did you? You just aren't good enough.

Both: Well, er, um, ah...

St Peter:	So in you go.
John:	I'm gonna be number one in there anyway.
James:	You mean I'm gonna be number one.
Mum:	Now hold on, boys. If we play our cards right, we can do big things in here.
	(They go in talking.)
St Peter:	Nice folks, but I can see I'm going to have some problems with them.
	(Blackout, accompanied by uproarious applause.)

QUESTIONS FOR DISCUSSION

Read Matthew 20:20-28.

1. Why did a mother make such a request?

2. What does Jesus mean in his reply in verse 22? What is the cup he speaks of? See Matthew 26:39.

3. They answer 'We can'. Compare this to Matthew 26:55-56.

4. Why is it not possible for unassisted humans to make it to heaven? (Romans 3:23; 6:23)

5. How, then, can we hope to spend eternity in the presence of God? (Romans 3:21-24; 1:16-17, and John 3:16-17)

6. Is it proud to believe we can earn our way into heaven? Does this mean we only have to believe, but not do anything? (James 2:14-20)

THE FAITH OLYMPICS

CHARACTERS:

Cringle Wolfensburger   Lot
Ron Fadeout

SCENE: *Music of sporting nature plays as sporting commentators carrying binoculars and clipboards enter with their chairs and adjust their microphones. When all are ready, music fades out.*

Cringle: Welcome, viewers, to another Saturday sports round up. This is Cringle Wolfensburger, and with me is Ron Fadeout...

Ron: Good afternoon.

Cringle: ...who'll be helping me with the commentating this afternoon. Well, today we are taking a look at the Faith Olympics being run on site in the Holy Land.

Ron: Yes and it looks like a fine afternoon of sporting highlights for the viewers. We have some really top class performers in these faith events...

Cringle: ... and I think we have the coverage of the first event, the leap of faith high jumps, ready right now. Would you care to comment... ?

Ron: Yes, thanks. Well, there is an impressive line up in this section with Abel, Abraham and Noah all competing. Abel is just taking his leap of faith with his perfect offering to God... and it's a beautiful jump with lots of form too.

(Sound of crowd cheering.)

Officials are measuring it up right now.

Cringle: And now I think it's Noah's leap of faith.

Ron: Yes and this is typical of his style too. Just look at the way he's building that ark even though all the neighbours are laughing at him.

Cringle: By jove yes, that man really has faith.

Ron: Oh but look at that leap Abraham took! He's leaving home! He's leaving his country!

Cringle: Good heavens! He's leaving everything, just because God told him to!

(Crowd cheering.)

Now that is a truly great leap, and, I think... yes, he has... Abraham has won his section with that great leap of faith.

(From off stage right, LOT shambles in, muttering.)

Lot: I told her not to, didn't I? I told her not to.

Cringle: Hey, who's that?

Ron: I don't know, but he shouldn't be here, should he?

Cringle: Hey, you! Old man! What are you doing here? Who are you, anyway!

Lot:	I'm Lot.
Cringle:	Lot?
Lot:	Lot.
Ron:	Well, that tells us a lot.
Lot:	And I told her a lot too. Lots of times I said to her, 'Don't look back'. That's what I said, don't look back, but would she listen? No, no, she just had to take a little peek, just had to see Sodom once more, just couldn't keep her eyes off it even though I kept telling her, 'Don't look back dear. Don't look back'. And now what is she? A pillar of salt, that's what she is. Just wouldn't listen when I said...
Cringle:	Yeah, yeah, all right, we get the picture, and we can't help it so...
Lot:	Help! You want to talk about help! What about me? Who's gonna help me do the dishes now, eh? Can't do 'em with a pillar of salt, can I, and what about the washing all lying round the tubs? What am I gonna do? Rub her on me sox to clean them or something? Are you gonna help me with the washing up? Are you? No. I didn't think so!
Cringle:	Ah look, get out of here, will you, this is on the air.
Lot:	Well, it's certainly on the nose.
	(Shambles off.)
Ron:	Now we turn to the water sports and we have two competitors listed here: Peter and Jonah... There's something fishy here.
Cringle:	Looks like they're having a whale of a time. Now if I can just interrupt a minute here. It seems Jonah has forfeited the event because... er... no one can find him.
Ron:	But it looks as if Peter is going to go ahead with it anyway just for the record attempt. And he's off and doing just fine, walking on that water.
Cringle:	Yes, it's a lovely sight too, five steps, six steps, he's...
	(Crowd cheering.)
	Oh dear. Oh.
	(They follow him down with their binoculars.)
	Oh, well. I guess he didn't listen to his coach enough.
	(Special delivery handed in.)
Ron:	Well... it looks like the women's events have been run and the results are here. Sarah took out the honours by having her baby at ninety years of age, and she won decisively over the other two competitors, Esther with her influencing of the Persian emperor; and Rahab the... ah... ummmm
	(Both cough and embarrassed.)
Lot:	*(Puts head in)* And my wife, don't forget her. I told her, 'Don't look..."
Cringle:	Will you get out of here!! We now have the coverage of the faith walking race which has already started and we pick it up on the home turn now,

and it's Enoch all the way. Really walking in faith. I think he has this race all sewn up.

(No cheer. They follow him up with their binoculars as he is taken up into heaven.)

Ron: Wow. What an exit!

Cringle: Well, it sure has been a day and a half in the other events too. Paul took out the foot races, running with patience the race God had set before him, and he also won the boxing, aiming his blows carefully and for fullest effect.

Ron: Well, that about completes the sports round up for this afternoon. I hope you've enjoyed the afternoon's viewing, and that you've been able to pick up some pointers for your own style.

Cringle: In the meantime, train hard, and it's good afternoon from Cringle Wolfensburger...

Ron: And from Ron Fadeout...

(Music plays in as they sit back to silently discuss or shuffle papers together as news readers do. Lights down to darkness. Exit.)

James and John cooperated successfully to almost complete the bobsled run at the Winter Faith Olympics.

QUESTIONS FOR DISCUSSION

BIBLE READINGS

Genesis 4:4
Genesis 6:9-22
Genesis 19:26
Matthew 14:22-32
Genesis 21:1-3
Jonah 1 and 2

Genesis 12:1-5
Joshua 2:1-14
Genesis 5:21-24
Hebrews 12:1
Philippians 3:12-14
1 Corinthians 9:24-27

QUESTIONS

1. What is faith? (Hebrews 11:1) Is faith blind or based on evidence? (Colossians 4:5-6: 1 Peter 3:15-16)

2. On what evidence do you base your faith?

3. Read Hebrews 11 for Paul's great exposition on faith? Are any of the characters in the play mentioned?

4. How does a person's faith show itself? (Matthew 7:15-20, Galatians 5:22-23, James 2:14-26)

5. How can we strengthen faith? Through Bible study? Study of historical and other facts? Prayer?

HAUNTING MIDNIGHT TALES

CHARACTERS:

Alfred Hitchcock	Dr Corpse
Offstage voice	Nurse Hearse
Undertaker	Newsreader

Alfred Hitchcock: And now, another night's horror and psychopathic fear for all you listeners out there.

(Screams, chains, torture chamber sound effects.)

Igor, close the door to *(local minister)*'s office, will you ?

Offstage voice: Yes master, heh heh heh.

(ALFRED HITCHCOCK character enters on stage.)

Alfred Hitchcock: No, *(name of a youth leader in your church.)* Not you, Igor will do it. As I was saying, it's another awful, horrific episode of Haunting Midnight Tales, stories of the macabre to curl your hair. Tonight we present 'Back From the Grave' - the story of bodies that just won't die.

Offstage voice: 'Back From the Grave' is brought to you by Vestinghouse, top name in home freezer units. If you want to come back from the dead, do it right and look your best.

Alfred Hitchcock: Good evening. Tonight, as the midnight hour approaches, our thoughts turn to the macabre, the paranormal, to hauntings, to grave stones, the paths of the dead, and (person or local TV show).

(Awful scream from offstage, long and drawn out.)

It's in the top drawer, dear, near the hankies. Tonight we examine the increasingly common phenomenon of the dead who return to walk again. The problem is grave. We look at the wide-ranging social and economic problems caused by this wave of people who walk again. Who could possibly profit from this haunted situation, except possibly the manufacturers of deodorants? Tonight we look closely at this crisis which is even now occurring at our front doors, and the casualties of this macabre and frightening return from the tomb. Speaking frankly, we don't stand a ghost of a chance.

(HITCHCOCK's side of the stage is darkened while he stays frozen and other side of stage opens in light to show undertaker's office with counter and the gentleman behind it. Phone on desk rings.)

Undertaker: Morning, Happy Corpse Funeral Directors and Undertakers, you die, we dig. Embalmed and ready in fifteen minutes. Coffin thrown in free, though most people prefer to be lowered. The Lazarus job? Yes, we did that one, and darned well too. Yes, the full treatment, bandages, coffin and all. Even sealed the grave with a big stone. That was four days ago now. What do you mean, is this an April Fool's Day joke? What?? You want your money

33

back? Well you were perfectly willing for us to wrap the guy up, comfort the mother and all that, weren't you? Well, look, if you can't guarantee that the guy's dead, you shouldn't have had him buried, should you? I don't care if he's walking down the road right now. He was dead when we buried him and you're not getting a refund. Well put your solicitor onto me then. Goodbye!! Ah this Jesus character going round bringing people back to life again. Boy, will I be glad when he dies so things can get back to normal again.

Alfred Hitchcock: *(Lights up on him and down on opposite scene.)* And so we can see the beginnings of these effects taking their toll on ordinary people. The dead are coming back again. They're spreading across the country and we aren't even aware of their ghostly presence. Go into any office building in town and you will find it's true. Witness the pallid faces, the glazed eyes, the blank facial expressions, the stench of decay and you'll know you've found the taxation office. What other areas of life and death could be affected? What about the medical field? Let's look at the latest episode of...

(Insert appropriate theme music.)

'The Young Morticians'. In this episode Doctor Corpse and Nurse Hearse are performing a delicate post mortem on the body of the late son of the widow of Nain.

(Lights fade on him again as operation table scene lights up on opposite side of stage.)

Dr Corpse: This is very delicate, nurse.

Nurse Hearse: Yes, doctor.

Dr Corpse: Give me the readings, nurse.

Nurse Hearse: Pulse rate, steady... steady on zero that is.

Dr Corpse: Respiration?

Nurse Hearse: Even... there is none.

Dr Corpse: Digestion?

Nurse Hearse: Eighteen.

Dr Corpse: Blood count?

Nurse Hearse: Four.

Dr Corpse: Pressure?

Nurse Hearse: Twenty-two.

Dr Corpse: BINGO!! And only on five calls too. Now to work.

Nurse Hearse: You're wonderful, doctor.

Dr Corpse: Yes. Now, forceps, retractor, swab, anaesthetic, pliers, scalpel. Now the incision must be made right... here.

(He cuts into body shape covered with sheet. There is long slow raspberry sound while what was apparently the corpse slowly deflates.)

Dr Corpse: Nurse, what was that sound?

Nurse Hearse: That was the sound of a blow up body going down, doctor.

Dr Corpse: And why is there a blow up body on this table and not the body of the widow of Nain's son?

Nurse Hearse: Because the widow's son was raised from the dead on the way over here and I didn't want you to miss your fun, doctor. Besides, I was hoping you'd ask me out to the freezer room attendants ball.

Dr Corpse: What?? Raising people from the dead? How am I going to make millions of dollars on false operations if this happens? Call the AMA quickly.

Nurse Hearse: But doctor, the freezer room attendants ball.

Dr Corpse: Who can think about dancing when my patients are being cured? It's outrageous!

(NURSE HEARSE emits a baby type wail)

(Scene fades to HITCHCOCK again.)

Alfred Hitchcock: And so you can see, the question of people being raised and returned unexpectedly from the dead has far-reaching implications, hasn't it? Of corpse it has! A little joke for those who like to laugh.

(Heavy breathy laughter.)

Gee I hate these tight collars. And now for the obituary notices.

(Light fades on HITCHCOCK and comes up on newsreader.)

Newsreader: And now we have the obituary notices. Relatives and friends of the late Joseph are requested by his family to join with them in a memorial service to be held in...

(Phone rings.)

Oh, I see. He's not really dead at all. A mistake. Right. Thank you.

(Replaces phone.)

Right, well, friends of the late daughter of Jairus are asked to attend her funeral and pay last respects to this young girl, tragically taken from us on...

(Phone rings again.)

Raised from the dead, eh? Right. Just go on then, shall I? Good.

(Replaces phone.)

Well in that case, friends and relatives of the late Eutychus, who was tragically killed in a fall from a window, are notified that...

(Phone rings again.)

Don't tell me. Right, I get the picture. Raised, eh? Right.

(Replaces the phone once again. Obviously frustrated.)

Well, in memory of the late Jesus of Nazareth, the family of the deceased have determined that...

(Phone rings again.)

Yes, yes, alright, I know all about it. Yes.

(Replaces phone. Sits miserably, sticks lower lip out and gives a quick sob.)

Not fair. They're all coming back.

Alfred Hitchcock: And so you can see, it's a real problem, you can be dead sure of that. With this spate of people returning, who knows, you may be the next to come back. So remember, just in case you do come back, be sure you're not buried in a see-through shroud. Well, that's all for tonight's episode of 'Haunting Midnight Tales'. We wish you all a good night's sleep. Remember, if you suffer from insomnia on these haunted nights, if sleep evades you and you toss and turn on your restless bed of agony, just listen to a tape of (insert name of local youth group leader or prominent person.) Remember that I personally recommend Comfy Coffin Cushions which are presented in an array of colours and are really plush and soft for that eternally comfortable feel. Comfy Coffin Cushions, you'll sleep best if we look after you. Good evening.

(Lights fade and curtains close.)

BIBLE READINGS

Relevant Bible readings on each incident are found in

John 11:1-11
Luke 7:11-17
Genesis 37:1-35
Mark 5:21-42
John 20:1 to 21:14

QUESTIONS FOR DISCUSSION

1. In what ways can death be seen as a final barrier?

2. Why have people always been so afraid of death?

3. Can death be seen as an end and a beginning?

4. In what way did the resurrection act as Jesus' final qualification or proof of his identity? (John 11:25 - note the context of this verse - Romans 1:2-4)

5. Many people can believe in Jesus as a prophet or a good man, but they draw the line at believing in the resurrection. Why? (Acts 17:32; Matthew 28:11-15)

6. How important to the Christian faith is the resurrection? (1 Corinthians 15:12-19)

Note   There are a number of excellent books which examine the logic and facts surrounding the resurrection. It would be well worth having a number of these on hand to examine some of the arguments, especially those which refute some of the alternate theories to explain the resurrection.

JOSEPH, THIS IS YOUR LIFE

CHARACTERS

Professor Time-bender   Mrs Potiphar
Joseph   Off stage voice
Six to ten extra characters to play various fill-in roles such as
brothers, slaves, Egyptians etc.

SCENE: *Curtain is closed for the voice over introduction.*

Voice over: This is your life, mate. Have you ever watched this show? Do you ever wonder why they never do it on people of the past and only on people of the present time zone? It makes it very dull, boring and lifeless. Of course, you can object, how could we interview someone who's dead? That would be even more lifeless. But let me tell you, it can be done because to us here at *(insert name of local T.V. station)*, time is no barrier. We sent our special agent back in time to interview a special character. Back thousands of years to an ancient world, to the land of the pharaohs.

(Curtain opens to reveal JOSEPH in typical Egyptian dancer position. PROFESSOR TIME-BENDER enters to theme music.)

Professor Time-bender: Er, hello. Are you Joseph?

Joseph: Yes, I am actually.

Professor Time-bender: Thought so. I've been looking for you. Strange that I should find you first out of the probable Egyptian population of some nine million, but then, these things can be done in cheap scripts. Well anyway, I'm Professor Time-bender, *bender, bender, time traveller. Together with my faithful companion what's her name, I traverse the bounds of time and space in a Westinghouse refrigerator carton in search of truth, rust and Neville the deranged robot.

Joseph: You are a very unbalanced man.

Professor Time-bender: But anyway folks, tonight, through the wonder of inter-stellar time zone travel, we bring you, Joseph, this is your life, mate.

Joseph: But you're not the usual guy who does this stuff.

Professor Time-bender: Quiet, smart aleck. Now Joseph, let's take you through your fondest memories of life with my little time warper here so the people out there in TV land can see it all happen before their very eyes. Now, stage one, you had eleven brothers, is that so?

Joseph: Yes, but...

---

*   See note about Time-bender's name on page 7.

"Ah... Excuse me Joseph. I know this is probably not a good time to ask, but ah... could you point me in the direction of Egypt?"

Professor Time-bender: Well, let's take you back to those good old days down on the farm.

Joseph: But wait on, I'm not too keen to go back and...

Professor Time-bender: Go to the time warper.

(JOSEPH enters the time warper. Strobe or faded light effect with a short burst of music sets the scene.)

Now as far as I can gather from the record here, you had eleven brothers and they all hated you.

(BROTHERS come on and begin to grumble and point at JOSEPH.)

They jeered at you...

(BROTHERS jeer. JOSEPH starts to look for a way of escape.)

They even beat you up...

(They mug JOSEPH.)

They carried you off...

(They carry him off stage.)

and threw you down a...

(Scream fades away from off stage.)

Er, is that right?

(Looks up from his book as JOSEPH comes crawling back on.)

Isn't it exciting? Then the next sound you heard was that of the tinkling of camel bells. Yes, it was the Ishmaelite slave traders coming along to buy you.

Joseph: Oh no, not that!

Professor Time-bender: Time warper again I think.

(JOSEPH steps into the time warper. Strobe and music again. As he exits, the camel drivers come in and drag JOSEPH away.)

Yes, that's right. They carried you off to Egypt and liberally beat you along the way.

(Whipping sounds offstage. Bidding, auctions, camels, etc.)

Ah, the typical Egyptian slave market. Here you were bought by a wealthy Egyptian nobleman called...

(Reads the narrative closer.)

What a name!! Pottifull, *(Laughs)*, Pottichair, *(Laughs louder)* No seriously, folks, his name was Potiphar.

(JOSEPH crawls on again.)

Is that right? And while you were there, you had a little trouble with Mrs Potiphar, is that also right?

Joseph: Oh no, please, anything but that.

(MRS POTIPHAR slinks on very seductively, dressed with beads, etc. and drapes herself over JOSEPH.)

Mrs Potiphar: Darrling, where have you been all my life? Here I am, rich, beautiful, bored and alone. There you are, young, handsome, active, strong, my dream come true. Oooo take me away, you big hunk.

Joseph: Look, lady, nick off.

Mrs Potiphar: Oh, don't break my heart with your cruel words. Take me before I faint.

(Tries to faint into his arms but he steps out of the way and she drops to the ground.)

Oh, boo hoo. Cast out by the arms of love. Speak to me, darrling. Say beautiful things into my ear.

Joseph: Go away.

Mrs Potiphar: Oh, it's like music.

(Grabs his ankles.)

Take me, I'm yours. I'll do anything you say...

Joseph: Go away.

Mrs Potiphar: ...except that.

Joseph: Look, you're a married woman and I'm not going to race off with you, so go and bother someone else.

Mrs Potiphar: You're not going to carry me away from all this?

Joseph: No.

Mrs Potiphar: *(Gets up.)* In that case... help, help. A virtuous woman has had liberties taken with her person.

Joseph: Huh?

(She races off screaming, then comes back and hands him part of her clothing.)

Mrs Potiphar: Here, hold this.

Joseph: Certainly.

Mrs Potiphar: He tore off part of my clothing.

(SLAVES with swords come in.)

Joseph: Oh no.

Mrs Potiphar: He attacked me. A married woman.

(Two slaves carry JOSEPH off while a third stays to comfort the gibbering MRS POTIPHAR.)

Mrs Potiphar: It was dreadful. I'm married and he tried to...

(Stops when she realizes slave also is male.)

Hi there, big boy. What are you doing tonight?

(Slave backs off and runs away followed by MRS POTIPHAR screaming after him to come back.)

Professor Time-bender: And so it's back to me. But Joseph, even while you were in prison, you did okay. You interpreted dreams. You said the king's butler was going to be...

(Offstage voice: 'Whooppee, I'm free!')

...and he was. You said the king's baker was going to be...

(Offstage strangled gargle)

...and you were right there too. You even got a good name with the pharaoh and eventually got to be grand vizier in charge of the whole country.

(JOSEPH crawls on again.)

Then your brothers came down to Egypt.

(BROTHERS come on.)

You revealed who you were, and they hugged and kissed you.

(They do so and mob JOSEPH.)

They brought your old man down too and he hugged and kissed you.

(It happens again.)

He brought down all your uncles and aunties and cousins and cats and dogs and sheep and cattle and they all hugged and kissed you.

(It happens with a great mob scene on stage.)

After all that, everything was all okay.

(Crowd separates to reveal JOSEPH swaying in centre stage, a wreck.)

Well, what have you got to say about your life after living it all again?

(JOSEPH collapses backwards.)

Professor Time-bender: And the moral of the story is, if you...

(Sound effect collage of time travel, theme music, mumbles and jeers, cattle, bells, whipping, screams, screams of rape, jail door, whooppee and gargle, family and crowd greeting and laughing, kissing, etc. plus any other effects you can find.)

...and keep trusting the Lord, you'll come out okay. Well, Joseph old mate, what do you think about it all? Life ain't that tough, is it?

(JOSEPH climbs to his feet.)

Joseph: You lunatic. I didn't want to go through all that again. *(Raves on angrily.)*

Professor Time-bender: Well, he seems a little bit upset so I think we'd better leave here and return to our own time, very quickly.

(Curtain, and music as PROFESSOR TIME-BENDER climbs into 'spaceship' and takes off with JOSEPH still after him.)

QUESTIONS FOR DISCUSSION

Highlights from Joseph's life can be found in Genesis 37 and Genesis 39 to 45.

1. How can the working of God's plan and purpose be seen in Joseph's life?

2. This story has served to comfort many who are suffering pain or disappointment. Why? (Genesis 50:15-20)

3. What other characters in the Bible endured much but had God's protection to see them through it in the end?

4. Genesis is a book which strongly emphasises God's promises. (See 28:10-15, 17:1-6, 12:1-3, 9:8-17.) What does the word covenant mean? (See also 1:27-30.)

5. Why is God continually involved in covenants and promises to humans; and why does God persist in contacting individuals and families?

Joseph sat high on the mountain top contemplating Pharaoh's dream. If he had been asked to interpret something about seven cows he would have known what to say, but what is the significance of seven prancing emus? Perhaps he should ask Pharaoh if he is certain they weren't seven ears of wheat.

PETER '92.

MAKE YOUR EXCUSE

CHARACTERS:

Quiz Master   King Solomon
Adam   Jeremiah
Sinful servant   Moses

SCENE: *Five chairs are set up in a row to form a quiz show format. The QUIZ MASTER is appropriately dressed, and carrying palm cards.*

Quiz Master: Good evening, ladies and gentlemen, and welcome to another episode of Make Your Excuse, television's richest talent quiz. This is where we put a panel of personalities on the spot and see how well they can get out of their responsibilities. Yes it's a quest for the excuse maker of the Old and New Testaments and we have a great line-up of contestants tonight. Ladies and gentlemen, will you welcome them with applause and acclamation as they come into the studio before our live audience.

Our first contestant is getting back to the original model, dressed exclusively by Big Bay Fig Orchards. It's Adam.

Representing the ordinary working person, we have the lazy servant of Matthew 25, the person with the one talent.

Into the realms of regal royalty and witty wisdom, we have King Solomon himself.

There's the youngest prophet ever to preach. Yes it is the weeping prophet, Jeremiah.

And finally, the man millions of ancient Egyptians came to know as *(raspberry sound)*, Moses.

You folks all know the rules of the game. I'll put a real life situation to you and you have to get out of it in a limited time by thinking up a legitimate excuse that our judges will pass. Meanwhile all you people at home can be thinking up your own excuses and maybe one day you will be one of our lucky guest panelists.

Now Contestant Number 1, Adam, are you ready?

Adam: Yes.

Quiz Master: Then think quick. Here is your situation. You have just committed the first sin the world has ever seen, thus dooming the entire human race to death and separation from God for the rest of time. Make your excuse, you have five seconds.

Adam: Um, Um, Um.

Quiz Master: Four, three, two.

Adam: Um, Um, she did it. Eve did it. She made me do it and it was all her fault.

Quiz Master: Yes, and it's a good excuse. You could be headed for the Grand Final, if you play Jackpot. Do you want to try and match the counter to your excuse?

Adam: Yes.

Quiz Master: Then here it is. You say Eve did it. The counter to that is... God warned you, in plain language, not to eat the fruit of the tree. How how do you get out of this? Make your excuse.

Adam: Um, um, um.

Quiz Master: Not fast enough I'm afraid, so it's on to the sinful servant. Right, Sinno, are you ready.

Sinful servant: Yes.

Quiz Master: Here it comes. All the other servants made sensible investments with their master's money and you didn't. Why? Make your excuse.

Sinful servant: Um, um, um.

Quiz Master: Five, four, three, two, one.

Sinful servant: Um I was too scared, so I buried the money.

Quiz Master: Not fast enough that time, I'm afraid.

Sinful servant: Oh bother.

Quiz Master: Now it's into the realms of the rich, with Solomon, richest king ever seen in the Holy Land and famed writer of the rudest book in the Old Testament. Are you ready, Your Majesty?

King Solomon: Ready, peasant.

Quiz Master: Then tell all the people listening, why did you marry hundreds of women from all the pagan nations of the known world including Moab, Ammon, Edom, and Egypt? Make your excuse. Five, four, three, two.

King Solomon: Um, um, um, I'm a masochist. I couldn't help myself. I like the ceremony. I like...

Quiz Master: I'm sorry, that's three excuses, not one and we'll have to disqualify you on that account.

King Solomon: I'll have you boiled in oil.

Quiz Master: I'm sorry, Kingo, that won't get you out of it. Rules are rules and I hate deep fried food. Now it's on to Jeremiah, the weeping prophet. Ready, Kiddo?

Jeremiah: Whahhhhh

Quiz Master: Then here it is, you have been charged to become God's spokesman to the world and tell them all how bad they really are. Make your excuse.

Jeremiah: I'm too young.

Quiz Master: A good answer and quick too, and the judges say 'yes'. You could be in the Grand Final. Do you want to play jackpot now or later?

Jeremiah: Whahhhhh.

Quiz Master:	Later, eh? Then it's on to the final contestant. And it's Moses, the man who goes around beating up Egyptian slave masters with pick handles. Now, Moses, are you ready?
Moses:	Yes, please.
Quiz Master:	Here it is, then. God has charged you with telling the Pharaoh to let the Israelites go. Make your excuse.
Moses:	They won't believe me. It's no good. No one would believe me and they'll say God never appeared to me.
Quiz Master:	And it's a swift answer from Moses. He gets the judges' approval. Do you want to risk it and play for jackpot which could automatically whizz you through to the Grand Final level?
Moses:	Yes, please.
Quiz Master:	Okay, then it's your funeral. They won't believe you, you say. But God says in counter to that... your staff is under supernatural control and you can turn it into a serpent at will. That's your proof. Make your excuse.
Moses:	I'm not a good speaker.
Quiz Master:	He's done it! A jackpot. Through to the Grand Final. Do you want to gamble and risk a double jackpot?
Moses:	Yes, please.
Quiz Master:	Wow, this guy is really going for it. This is excuse making at its best, ladies and gentlemen. Okay, here comes your next situation. Have your pep pills handy. The Lord says, 'I can give you the words to say' so it matters not that you cannot speak well. Make your excuse.
Moses:	Please don't send me. I just don't want to go. I really don't... Please.
Quiz Master:	He's done it. The judges say yes, a double jackpot from that beaut set of excuses. He walks right into the winnings for this series. Moses, come right up here and get your prize money.
Moses:	Ah no, man. It's a long way there and I've got a sore foot.
Quiz Master:	Come up here now, please.
Moses:	No, I'm bashful.
Quiz Master:	Will you stop making excuses and get up here? We're on air, you know.
Moses:	Aw, I've got a cold. My car broke down. My mother won't let me. I had a bad childhood. All my brothers hated me and I got a rejection complex.

(Lights fade out as they argue and quiz music plays)

QUESTIONS FOR DISCUSSION

BIBLE READINGS

Stories and incidents referred to in the play can be found in:

> Genesis 3:8-13
> Matthew 25:14-30
> 1 Kings 11:1-8
> Jeremiah 1:4-5
> Exodus 3:1 to 4:17

QUESTIONS

1. What excuses have you offered to God to try to escape a task it is obvious you must do?

2. In the cases of Moses and Jeremiah, God was still able to use these men for great works. Is it possible, however, to make ourselves unusable, even to God?

3. What talents, skills or gifts has God given you? Why do people tend to say, 'God hasn't given me any real talents or gifts'. Is this an excuse?

4. Make a list of all the things that people in the group can competently do. Include such daily skills as driving a car, gardening, sewing, talking, etc. How can these be used to help others in the name of Jesus?

5. Considering the following: Matthew 9:35-38; John 5:15-17 and John 9:4-5. Is there any reason for someone to feel unwanted or useless?

SO YOU WANNA GO BACK TO EGYPT

CHARACTERS

Moses	Ishmael
Aaron	Fanmail
Habakkuk	Airmail
Mrs Kuk	Voice offstage

SCENE   *Opens with play over of suitable music, for example a song concerning the Israelites in Egypt or the wilderness. As lights come up on a restaurant scene, Mannacake Manor advertisements may be flashed up onto OHP screens either side of the stage or above, if such can be rigged up. These signs should be recognisably similar to some well known local eating houses's advertisements. AARON is present onstage, dusting off the seating mats or tables if there are such.*

Moses: All ready, Aaron?

Aaron: Yes sir, Mr Moses.

Moses: Table cloths all in order?

Aaron: Yes, sir.

Moses: Aaron, bring up the lights a little. Don't want it too dark, do we, yet still with a romantic atmosphere.

Aaron: Yes sir, Mr Moses.

Moses: Menus must go out.

Aaron: Do you really think it's necessary, Mr Moses? I mean, most of the customers for this restaurant are regulars. They know our food.

Moses: No, we must keep up our good image. After all, we are the best restaurant in these parts.

Aaron: Well, it all seems to be set. Only a couple of minutes to the morning serving.

Moses: Yes, as a matter of fact, our regular customers, Habakkuk and his family are due at any moment.

(On the other side of the stage HABAKKUK and his family enter as MOSES and AARON bustle about.)

Mrs Kuk: Well, dear, here we are.

Habakkuk: Yes, dear. Are all the children in order? Children?

Children: Yes, abba.

Habakkuk: Abba! I told you kids to stop listening to those punk rock groups.

Mrs Kuk: No, dear. Abba is Hebrew for father.

Habakkuk: Oh, yes. I keep forgetting. After all, we only came out of Egypt a few decades ago.

Mrs Kuk:	Now, children, all in order. We want you to look neat when we go out. Ishmael, Fanmail, Airmail. Good, that's better.
Habakkuk:	Morning, Aaron.
Aaron:	Ooh, look. They're here.
Moses:	I'll go see to the kitchen.
Aaron:	Morning, Habakkuk, Mrs Kuk and all the little Kuks, the typical ancient Hebrew family. Eating area for five as usual?
Habakkuk:	Yes, thank you. Just one thing, though, Aaron. As you know, we've been coming here for the last thirty years, and tonight we observed that someone had parked their camel in our usual lot.
Aaron:	Lot? Lot? What's he doing here? It's too late in the Bible for him. He hasn't been round since Genesis.
Mrs Kuk:	No, not that Lot. The parking lot. There's someone else's camel in our parking lot.
Aaron:	Oh, sorry. It must be someone from the take-away section. Don't worry. We'll look after that.
	(AARON shows them to their seating mats where they all sit.)
Aaron:	May I recommend the soup of the day? It's a very nice cream of manna, or perhaps you prefer the manna paté?
Habakkuk:	Will you be having entree, dear?
Mrs Kuk:	Well, the manna kilpatrick looks nice, but I've had that for the last thirty years.
Habakkuk:	Well, I think I might have the manna on horseback. Why don't you try the fresh manna cocktail, dear?
Mrs Kuk:	Children, what would you like today? Why don't you have some mannabert cheese with mannavite crispbreads.
Ishmael:	We don't want manna, dad.
Fanmail:	Can we have porky spareribs, dad, can we, huh huh huh?
Habakkuk:	No you cannot have porky spareribs!
Airmail:	Oh why not?
Mrs Kuk:	Because it's ceremonially unclean, that's why.
Ishmael:	Aw, the Moabite kids down the road are allowed to eat pork all the time. Why can't we?
Habakkuk:	When you're older you'll understand. Eat what you're given and that way you'll make it into the kingdom of heaven. So mind your manners.
Mrs Kuk:	Oh look, dear. It says, 'Fresh fruit when in season'. *(To AARON)* I'll have some of that, please.
Aaron:	I'm sorry, it isn't in season.
Habakkuk:	Well, let's not have entrees. Let's look at the main meals.

Mrs Kuk:	Look. There's manna diane.
Ishmael:	And manna in a basket.
Fanmail:	And manna burgers.
Airmail:	And manna in a hole.
Habakkuk:	And manna chasseur. Haven't you got anything without manna in it?
Aaron:	Well, actually, no.
Mrs Kuk:	But we've ben coming here for the last thirty years and the menu hasn't changed.
Aaron:	Well, I'm sorry, but the cook seems to think that this is best for you.
Mrs Kuk:	Isn't there anything else we can eat besides manna?
Voice over:	Would the owner of a beige-coloured camel with twin bucket humps and Edomite registration plates please remove this vehicle or it will be towed away?
Children:	*(General whinging breaks out.)*
Habakkuk:	Quiet, or I'll take you out and lock you in the camel.
Mrs Kuk:	I think this is absolutely disgusting. Here we are. Regular customers. And this is all they have for us.
Habakkuk:	We've had manna day and night. I don't even want to *hear* that word again. Where's the manager? Oh, no! I said it again.
Aaron:	I'll go and get Mr Moses.
	(AARON exits hurriedly to get Mr MOSES. They re-enter in a business-like fashion.)
Moses:	Good morning, Habakkuk and Mrs Kuk. Is there any way I can be of service?
Habakkuk:	Yes, you can. You can organise this restaurant a bit better and provide us with some decent food. Don't you have any notion of what it is to give the customer variety? What sort of manager are you? You're supposed to be feeding us and all we get is manna day and night. Your cuisine shows about as much imagination as *(insert name of popular song artist)*'s lyrics.
Mrs Kuk:	In fact, if it wasn't for one little problem, we'd go somewhere else.
Aaron:	And what's the problem?
Mrs Kuk:	There *is* nowhere else.
Habakkuk:	Can't you order from a different supplier or something?
Aaron:	But this supplier has never let us down all these years.
Moses:	Anyway, the chef does all the ordering. It's not only us you're complaining about, it's the chef. And that's not a wise move.
Fanmail:	But all he does is make manna all the time.
Airmail:	I hate manna. Manna's yukky.

Ishmael:	Why can't we have a hamburger.
Fanmail:	Fish and chips.
Airmail:	Pizza.
Moses:	Well, we could go and see the chef about it, but it's not advisable to complain to our chef.
Habakkuk:	Just go and tell him we want something else.
Mrs Kuk:	And while you're at it, we may as well make a list of all the other things we've been going to complain to Moses about for years. I, for one, am sick of living in a tent.
Habakkuk:	Well, lose some weight and I'll buy you a proper dress!
Mrs Kuk:	Shut up! Have you any idea what it's like to live in a tent with a sand floor? Do you know what that does to a vacuum cleaner? Last week I vacuumed till I was four metres deep and I still couldn't get rid of the sand.
Ishmael:	And the sand's hot on your feet.
Airmail:	And there's always sand in your sleeping bag.
Fanmail:	And nobody really knows where we're going.
Whole family:	And we're sick of manna!
Habakkuk:	We were better off in Egypt.
Moses:	Alright then. I'll go and see what the chef has to say about it.
Aaron:	*(On the way out.)* I'll just turn the television on for you so you can watch it and take your mind off all this business about manna.
	(On the OHP screen appear various weather maps of the Middle East.)
Voice over:	And now the weather report. Over the past twenty-four hours, there were good falls of manna recorded in the Desert of Sin which is between Elim and Sinai. The area recorded one hundred millimetres of manna in the six hours to three o'clock this afternoon. Falls were so heavy in places that the manna ploughs had to be brought out to clear roads and traffic...
Habakkuk:	*(Who has been growing increasingly agitated.)* Enough! Turn it off.
Mrs Kuk:	Wonder who the chef is, anyway?
	(MOSES and AARON return.)
Moses:	We've talked to the chef and the chef says you are free to eat anything else you like and that you don't have to eat manna any more.
	(Whole family cheers and rushes for the door. At the door, they suddenly stop as the realisation hits them. They return quietly to the eating area.)
Habakkuk:	There *is* nothing out there.
Mrs Kuk:	Only desert.
Ishmael:	Sand.
Fanmail:	Rock.

Airmail:	Camel manure.
Aaron:	Yes, we know.
Mrs Kuk:	We'd die if we tried to live off the land.
Moses:	Yes, there is that fact.
Habakkuk:	Perhaps we shouldn't complain about the chef so much. Er, who is the chef?
Aaron:	God.
	(Silence.)
Mrs Kuk:	God! You mean the 'no other Gods besides me' type God?
Habakkuk:	I suppose we should be more appreciative, seeing God provided it for us.
Moses:	And isn't it God who's been looking after us all this time ?
Whole family:	Well...
Aaron:	Who got us out of slavery in Egypt?
Whole family:	God.
Moses:	Who gave us water from the rock when we needed it?
Whole family:	God.
Aaron:	Who gave us victory over the Amalekites?
Moses:	And brought us quails to eat?
Aaron:	And led us with pillars of fire and smoke?
Habakkuk:	Let us give thanks for the food we have been given.
	(Family reverently join hands, bow their heads for grace. Blackout.)

The ants knew that there was no way they could get to promised land during the exodus without hitching a ride.

PETER '92.

QUESTIONS FOR DISCUSSION

A background knowledge of the period of slavery in Egypt, and the leading out by Moses will be of benefit here. Various examples of the people's complaints can be seen in Exodus 14:5-12; 15:22-25; 16:1-3; 17:1-3 and Numbers 14:1-10.

1. Read Exodus 16:1-35. What, in verses 17-20, shows how little human nature has changed?

2. Compare the extra information given in the account in Numbers 11:4-9. What ways of preparing manna were used to give some variety?

3. What did the manna taste like when fresh (Exodus 16:31)? Why did people get sick of it? What alternative food supplies were there?

4. Even Moses himself complained to the Lord (Number 11:10-15). Compare this to Exodus 3:9 to 4:16; 1 Kings 19:1-14, Jeremiah 15:10-18 and Matthew 26:36-46. Have you done a similar thing? When?

5. Is it alright to complain to the Lord, or to get angry at God?

6. What was God's reaction to these people when they complained?

NICODEMUS

CHARACTERS:

Nicodemus   Jesus
Child
A miscellaneous crowd of party-goers including three speaking
parts: Party-goer 1
Party-goer 2   Party-goer 3
A couple of passers-by and spare persons, non-speaking parts.

SCENE: *Stage is in semi-darkness. Sneaky piano or other music plays as NICODEMUS tip toes on from upstage left and moves to downstage left. CHILD enters from opposite side and NICODEMUS calls him over.*

Nicodemus: Psst. Hey, kid. Come over here. Wanna earn yourself a shekel?

Child: Mum told me about weirdo's like you, mister.

Nicodemus: No, listen...

Child: You'll only throw me into a car and kidnap me. There's a safety synagogue near here and I'm going to...

Nicodemus: Look, shut up! I can't throw you into a car. It's 33 A.D. and they haven't been invented yet.

Child: Oh, well, this is stranger danger week at school and... hey, wait on. You're no stranger. I know you, you're really famous round here. You're Nicodemus.

Nicodemus: Shhh! Shut up! Now listen. Go over to that house. *(Indicating downstage right)* Knock on the door and ask for a man named Jesus. Don't say I'm here. Don't say anything about me. Just tell him to stand at the door.

Child: Okay.

(CHILD goes to imaginary door downstage right and knocks. Person comes out. They speak and person disappears and JESUS comes out. CHILD points across to stage left where NICODEMUS is standing. NICODEMUS takes out a torch and begins to flash a morse code message. JESUS considers a moment, then takes out his own torch and flashes a message back.)

Nicodemus: Good, here comes a reply. *(Reading the signals.)* It is improper for a Jewish leader to be seen on the streets flashing. Darn!

Child: *(Calls loudly.)* It's okay, Nicodemus! You can come over now!

Nicodemus: *(Tearing his hair out and racing across.)* Shhh!! Quiet!! Look, I'm a leader of the Sanhedrin, and I must not be seen here, and people must not know why I've come. Here, kid. Take this shekel and nick off.

Child: That's a good one. Nick off, Nicodemus. Hee hee. *(Runs off.)*

Nicodemus: Now, rabbi.

Jesus: *(Has been rather enjoying the joke. He becomes serious again.)* Yes?

Nicodemus:	Are we alone?
Jesus:	Well I'm not.
Nicodemus:	*(Gasp.)* Who's with you?
Jesus:	You.
Nicodemus:	Oh yes. Well, rabbi, we know you are a teacher from... er... God. No one could do the miracles you do unless... er... God was with him.
Jesus:	I'm telling you the truth. No one can see the kingdom of God unless that person is born again.
	(Passer-by enters from opposite side and crosses stage.)
Nicodemus:	*(Seeing person coming.)* Shhh! Yes, sir, this genuine anti-static camel hair brush is what you need. It will save you big bucks in dry cleaning bills. For just five shekels, yes five shekels... *(sees person is gone)*... what was that you were saying?
Jesus:	You must be born again.
Nicodemus:	*(Yells)* What?? Shhh! I mean, what? How can I be born again? I can't, you know, get back into... you know ... *(another passer-by is coming)* Shhh! Give to the lifesavers, sir. The Sea of Galilee Surf Lifesaving Club needs your help. I mean, what would you do if you were out on the sea and a storm blew up?
Jesus:	I'd tell the waters to be still.
Nicodemus:	Shhh! Yes. Yes. Quite. Well, as I was saying. What do you mean, born again? My mother would be horrified! The woman's ninety-three years old. Don't you think it might be a bit... well... uncomfortable?
Jesus:	No, no, no. Don't be surprised when I say you must be born again. A person is born physically of human parents, but is born spiritually of the Spirit.
Nicodemus:	What? How do you figure that one?
Jesus:	Aren't you supposed to be a great teacher in this country? Surely you should be able to figure that out. I mean, if you don't understand when I use simple parallels from this world, how will you understand when I talk about things from heaven?
Nicodemus:	But listen...
	(A group of party-goers enters from upstage centre or upstage left.)
Nicodemus:	Oh, no! Here come a mob of people. Someone may recognise me. Look, this is a very interesting theological concept you have here, being born again and all that. I'll have to catch up with you some time about it.
Party-goer 1:	Hey, look, boys! It's Nicodemus. Hey, Nic. Who's that you're talking to?
Nicodemus:	Oh, no one. Just asking directions.
Party-goer 2:	Well, come on with us and we'll show you the way home.
Party-goer 3:	*(Sings drunkenly.)* Show me the way to go home...
Nicodemus:	Come on, quieten down. That's no way for an Israelite to behave.

Party-goer 3: Sorry.

Party-goer 1: Come on, then.

Nicodemus: Look, Jesus. You get out of sight. I'll catch up with you later on. How about in a couple of weeks, after the Passover?

(He starts to exit towards stage left trying to look nonchalant with the mob.)

Nicodemus: *(To JESUS)* Have a good Passover.

Jesus: *(Waits till they are gone, then replies quietly.)* And you have a good Easter.

(Blackout.)

Nicodemus had absolutely no concerns about being seen talking to Jesus.

QUESTIONS FOR DISCUSSION

1. See John 3:1-12. We have been a little uncharitable to Nicodemus in this play. It is possible he came by night because he was afraid to be seen talking to Jesus. However, it may have just been that he wanted a long talk. Why would this not have been possible during the day? See Matthew 9:1-8.

2. See John 3:5. This verse has been variously interpreted. Compare Titus 3:5 and John 1:31 and 3:22. What is your conclusion?

3. What is Jesus telling Nicodemus here? Note he uses and all-inclusive 'you' in John 3:7 and the word 'must' is a command.

4. See John 3:3, and note that the Greek can also be translated 'born from above'. Is this translation still consistent with Jesus' message? Does it make it any clearer to you? Why?

5. If you were to be born again, what aspects of your personality profile would you change? Is it possible to ask God to change them?

NOAH AND THE TUBES

CHARACTERS

Voice over	Japheth
Shem	Mrs Noah
Noah	Bikie 1
Ham	Bikie 2

SCENE: *While the curtain is still closed, a Voice over character reads the start of the Old Testament Noah story. This fades out as a suitable 'surfing' tune is turned up louder. The curtain opens and NOAH is revealed standing surveying the beach, which is in the direction of the audience. He is standing, arms folded, eyes squinting in the imagined glare and pointing at surf.*

Shem: Father.

Noah: What is it, Shem?

Shem: What are you doing?

Noah: I'm surveying the scene for tubes, you know, waves, swell, breakers and all that deal.

Shem: You can't do that here, father.

Noah: Yes, I can.

Shem: No, you can't.

Noah: Why not?

Shem: Because we're in the middle of the Mesopotamian Desert, that's why.

Noah: Oh no, I heard just this morning...

(HAM and JAPHETH come in, rocking and singing to surf music.)

Hey you guys, hang in there, there's gonna be tube city here soon. Nine foot swell, maybe more.

(Cheers from others.)

Shem: Wait on, wait on. How come there's gonna be tubes and pipelines here in the middle of the desert?

Noah: Didn't you hear the surf report on the radio this morning? It said big waves right here.

Japheth: What radio? They ain't been invented yet, dad.

Noah: Well someone told me. I heard a deep voice saying, 'Big waves. Lots of water. Great shore breaks all along here'. *(Thinks about that statement a bit.)* You mean that wasn't the weather reporter?

Ham: Wait on. A deep voice, from up above, predicting the future.

(Slowly all gaze above and drop to their knees.)

Noah: Thanks for the surf report, Lord.

Ham:	This'll really blow 'em away at the temple.
Shem:	Heavy duty stuff, eh?
Japheth:	Wow, a message from the real weather reporter.
	(All climb to their feet.)
Noah:	The Lord also dropped in all this really good detail on the shape of the break and the right type of board to build. We build one board 300 feet long and wax down with tar.
Ham:	Wow, 300 feet long.
Shem:	That's gonna be some swell, man.
Japheth:	There's got to be a catch.
Noah:	There is, boys. We gotta take two of every animal with us.
Ham:	Even mum?
Noah:	Yeah, man, we gotta take mum.
Shem:	Ah gee.
Japheth:	Couldn't we just pack an extra gorilla?
Noah:	Come on, boys, enough of this talk, we've got real work to do. We're all gonna hang ten off this mega board when the tubes come our way.
All boys:	Yeah, man, walk the plank, ride the hook, wipe out to the max.
	(Start building. Heavy bikie rock and roll as the guys in black leather enter.)
Bikie 1:	Hey, look at the dumb dudes over there.
Bikie 2:	Hey, weirdos, watcha doin'?
Ham:	Oh no. It's the town heavies.
Shem:	Hey cool it, you guys.
Japheth:	Yeah, we don't want no heavy aggro scenes here.
Bikie 1:	Hey, you dudes got brine on the brain or something? Watcha doin'?
Noah:	Aw nothin'.
Bikie 2:	Looks like some kinda giant surfboard, man.
	(All surfies respond in uproar saying, 'What, where, who, I don't see anything', etc.)
Bikie 1:	There, behind you, man. The 300 foot long one.
Noah:	Aw that. *(Laughs.)*
Ham:	We better tell 'em, daddyo.
Bikie 2:	Well?
Noah:	The Lord told us there's big tubes coming.
	(BIKIES roar with laughter.)
Bikie 1:	Ah come on, you guys, you been sniffing seaweed again or something?

Bikie 2:	Grow a brain, man. This is the desert. Why don't youse get bikes or something?
Shem:	But there's tubes coming.
Bikie 1:	Ah pull your head in!

(MRS NOAH enters, yelling.)

Mrs Noah:	Noah. Noah!! *(Gasp)* Bikies, attacking my boys!

(Begins to chase them around the stage.)

You greasy no hopers, how dare you attack a poor little defenceless lady who can't look after herself and is too weak to be left alone. Get out of here, you creeps, before I...

(They exit quickly and MRS NOAH turns and comes back to the others.)

Noah!!

(Pulls him up by the ear from where he is huddled, trying to hide from her.)

Noah:	Yes, dear?
Mrs Noah:	I don't know why I put up with you. Do you know what I found when I opened the fridge for a cold drink this morning? Well, do you?
Noah:	No, dear.
Mrs Noah:	Penguins! And a walrus fell out of the freezer. And what are we meant to wash in round here? I go up to the bath and find it's full of crocodiles, and there's a hippo in the handbasin.
Noah:	Yes, dear.
Mrs Noah:	And that's not all... you remember the two rabbits you put under the bed? Well there's 500 of them now. They've ruined the lettuce patch and there's a giraffe with his head stuck up the chimney and the carpets are covered with 4,000 different kinds of ants.
Noah:	I told those ants we only wanted two. They never listen.
Mrs Noah:	I haven't finished yet. When I turn the TV on to watch 'Days in our Desert', all I see is the wombat that's built its nest in there!
Noah:	Won't be long now, dear.
Mrs Noah:	And when are you going to do something about that rotten skunk that sits in my favourite arm chair? He just sits there and grins at me. I never know what he's going to do next.
Ham:	What's for lunch, mum?
Mrs Noah:	Nothing. And do you know why? Because your father put the tigers in the larder and they've gone and eaten everything. Not only that, the cat is terrified of the wolves in the laundry basket and the buffalo keep messing up the back yard.
Shem:	But it's good compost for the garden, mum.
Mrs Noah:	What garden? The back yard is full of kangaroos, koalas and zebras.

Japheth: Better get the washing in, mum, it's starting to rain.

Mrs Noah: What washing! I hung it all out yesterday and the Swiss mountain goats ate the lot, even my six pairs of bloomers.

Noah: They must have been very very hungry, dear.

Mrs Noah: And you boys are just as bad as your father. You think of nothing but your rotten surf boards. Well I suppose I'd better get back to it then. I've got to get that skunk off the chair.

(Exits as the others looks towards the sky and put out their hands to test for rain.)

Noah: Hey, man, it's starting to rain.

Ham: Yeah, we finished just in time.

Shem: Get them animals in.

Japheth: Gee, I wonder if mum got rid of that skunk.

(MRS NOAH screams offstage and rushes, screaming, across stage holding her nose.)

Noah: No, I don't think she did.

(All mime herding the animals in. Bikies enter again and NOAH talks to them while rest of family is getting animals into ark.)

Bikie 1: Hey, man, what is this, a new zoo or something?

Bikie 2: Wow, baby, with all them animals around, youse guys is gonna smell even worse than you usually do.

(They roar with laughter.)

Noah: Hey, you guys wanna come too? Look, you can surf with us. This whole place is gonna be solid water soon.

Bikie 1: You kiddin' me, man?

Bikie 2: Yeah, we got more important things to do. There's this big hill climb coming up.

(Exit. There is the effect of rain and thunder, as lights dim and all characters move off stage in opposite direction to where bikies exit.)

Voice over: And it rained and rained. And the floods came up and covered the face of the earth. Above the sounds of a drowned world and the cries of sinful people, and as the last traces of that disgusting race were wiped from the planet, there was heard the pure voice of prophecy; the last remnant of righteous humanity.

All: *(From offstage)* Whee, look at me, baby, hang ten. There's a big set coming. Wow, cool baby. *(And similar refrains.)*

(Fade out with surfing music.)

QUESTIONS FOR DISCUSSION

Genesis 6:5 to 8:22. There seem to have been two versions of this very ancient story, which have been woven into the one account. Note 7:1-3.

1. What does the account show of Noah's obedience, faith and personality?

2. Make a scale drawing of the boat, with a two metre human figure next to it to give some idea of its size.

3. How does this story show God's concern for the human race, for animals and for the world in general?

4. Who closed and sealed the ark? Genesis 7:16

5. The water of the flood was not just rain water. Where else did it come from?

6. What would have been the likely reaction of local people to Noah's building project?

7. Compare the simple statement of Genesis 7:5 with Genesis 3:10-13, 4:8-9. See also Jeremiah 1:4-6 and Jonah 1:1-3.

For one panic stricken moment, Noah wondered if the elephant would remember the word "stop!".

RELIGIOMART

CHARACTERS

Manager
Religious songs assistant
Religious festivals assistant
Burnt offerings assistant
Grain offerings assistant
Wailer 1
Wailer 2

Customer 1
Customer 2
Customer 3
Messenger
Union representative
Voice over

SCENE: *The stage may be in darkness or merely empty.*

Voice over: Amos 5:16-17. And so the Lord Almighty says: 'There will be wailing and cries of sorrow in the streets. Even farmers will be called to mourn the dead along with those professional wailers who are paid to mourn. There will be wailing in the streets. And this will take place because I am coming to punish you'. The Lord has spoken.

Scene: Religiomart, the biggest hire centre for religious equipment in the Middle East.

(Lights may come up here. ASSISTANTS run on and form into a tableau for the song. If lights have been down, ASSISTANTS may have been already onstage waiting.)

Assistants: *(Chanting or singing to any tune which fits the rhythm.)*
Do you want to please the Lord?
Making sure of your reward,
Just getting ready for the judgement day,
Being good and feeling holy.
We've got offerings to buy and songs to use.
Festive occasions from which you can choose
Let Religiomart get you in good with the Lord.
Religiomart will keep you holy.

Manager: *(Entering briskly.)* Right, everyone, pay attention, please. It's nearly nine o'clock here at Religiomart, and we always open on time. But first, I want a word with you. Our Religiomart market analysts have informed us that the news is true. The day of the Lord is coming. Naturally, we must all be ready and fully equipped for the big rush on our products. People are lining up outside already and they're really keen to hire our religious equipment. They're very concerned to ensure that they're doing the right thing when the Lord comes and we at Religiomart can help them with our wide range of artifacts, equipment and consultancy services.

All: Hear hear!

Manager: Now, in the Religious Songs, Hymns and Harps Department, are you all tuned up? Lots of people are going to want religious music.

Songs assistant: We're ready.

Manager: Now there's going to be a big demand for offerings in all forms. So what have we there?

Grain offerings: Well, in the Grain Offerings Section, we've got in a whole shipload of grains for the grain offerings. There are eight diferent types including organically grown and unsprayed grains for the health fanatics.

Burnt offerings: And in the Burnt Offerings Section we have, caged and ready, all manner of cows, bulls, goats, pigeons. Plenty for everyone and each animal is branded with a lucky number. We draw the winner this arvo and they win a free seat on top of the temple on the day of the Lord to see all the Gentiles and foreigners getting punished.

All: Hear hear!

Manager: What about the Religious Festivals Department?

Religious festivals: Well, we have a wide range of festivals available, all run by professional singers, dancers and chefs. We're all geared up and ready for the big rush.

All: Hear hear!

Manager: That's wonderful. Well, today we...

Wailer 2: What about us?

Manager: Who are you?

Wailer 1: The Wailing Department.

Manager: Oh, yes. Wailing. I suppose there'll be a couple of funerals where professional wailers will be needed. That's about all, though.

Wailer 2: Is that all? We've just worked out some really great new routines. Listen to this. *(To WAILER 1)* Let's do the new funeral number we rehearsed yesterday.

(They go into a rhythmic series of bursts of wailing which becomes easily recognisable as some well known piece of music done in wailing, for example Beethoven's Fifth Symphony.)

Manager: *(Interrupting.)* Yes, yes. That's fine, but you see, there isn't going to be very much call for you, I'm afraid. Once the day of the Lord comes, all wailing will cease. Actually, with that in mind, I've been going to make an announcement to you all. We're going to open a new Rejoicing Department that will cater for all the partying that will occur when the day of the Lord comes and all the Gentiles and sinners are punished. As a matter of fact, you wailers will be transferred to the new department, starting with you.

Wailer 1: But I like wailing!

Manager: Then you'll just have to retrain!

Both wailers: *(Bursting into tears.)* Wahhhhh!

Manager: Don't practise in here! Now, it's nine o'clock. Behind your counters, everyone. I'll start checking the plans for the new Rejoicing section.

(MANAGER moves to upstage where he wanders round planning quietly to himself and measuring things up. He should be inconspicuous so as not to attract attention to himself and away from the source of action downstage. All the ASSISTANTS move to their counters as the doors are opened off stage and customers race noisily in and begin examining catalogues, talking quietly, etc. CUSTOMER 1 goes to the Religious Festivals section.)

Customer 1: Hello, I'd like to have a religious festival, please.

Religious festivals: Certainly, sir. Which one would you like?

Customer 1: I don't know. Any one! I want to get in good before the Lord comes. Which one are we due for? How about the Passover?

Religious festivals: *(Looking at a calendar.)* No, we've already had that one.

Customer 1: How about Christmas?

Religious festivals: Never heard of it.

Customer 1: How about that one when we all go camping. What is it again?

Religious festivals: The Festival of Shelters.

Customer 1: That's the one. I'll take it.

Religious festivals: Good, now here's the voucher. Take that out the back to the man in overalls and he'll load up your camel.

Customer 1: Great. Thanks. Here's the money. *(Confidentially.)* I got it by refusing to pay my farm labourers their wages.

(They both laugh.)

I feel holier already. *(Exits.)*

Manager: (In the background talking on to himself.)

Customer 2: *(At the Religious Songs Department.)* Hello. What have you in the way of religious songs that will impress the Lord?

Religious songs: Well, what sort of song would you like?

Customer 2: Something quiet, sensitive and meditative, praising the Lord's goodness to me.

Religious songs: Has the Lord been good to you?

Customer 2: Certainly has. I mean, the Lord sent me a great opportunity just this morning. I was about to cross the road when I saw a little old lady standing there, waiting by the busy road.

Religious songs: And?

Customer 2: And I robbed her. Here, the money will help me buy the right song.

(CUSTOMER 2 pays and exits and MANAGER speaks to himself again.)

Manager: And this old Wailing Department area can be renovated to become the store room for the new Rejoicing Department. We'll put shelves over there and... *(He exits, talking.)*

Customer 3:   Good morning. What do you have in the way of offerings? I'm due for my weekly sin offering to keep me holy for when the day of the Lord comes.

Grain offerings: Well, if you want grain offerings, we have a wide range.

Burnt offerings: And we have animals waiting to be sacrificed.

Grain offerings: Of course, if you'd like to do the whole thing yourself, we have sacrifice kits available, with full instructions.

Burnt offerings: However, if your time is short, we have them ready cooked to take away and put straight on your altar.

Grain offerings: Tastefully prepared by competent chefs.

Burnt offerings: Our bar-be-que chicken is prepared with eleven different herbs and spices and can be served with garlic bread. But if you're looking for something like a sacrificial bull in herbs with salad, we have a special package deal named after one of our famous prophets. It's called the Big Zac.

Customer 3:   I'll take two of them. Boy, will my altar have a great sacrifice on it today! And throw in a large fries and a locusts and honey thickshake.

Burnt offerings: *(Holding microphone very close to mouth.)* Two big zacs, fries, thickshake flavour L and H. Pick up your sacrifices at the first window, have a good evening.

(CUSTOMER 3 pays and goes off to collect.)

Manager: *(Enters.)* Oh, boy. We'll have the best Rejoicing Department in the land ready for the day of the Lord. Oh what joy that will be when we are able to close down that dingy old Wailing Department.

(MESSENGER enters.)

Messenger: Hey, everybody! Guess what? The day of the Lord is here! It's come. Get ready for it!

Manager: What? Here already! It's come earlier than we thought. Quickly, you in the Wailing Department, get over to the Festivals Department. No. On second thoughts, go to the Songs Department. People will really be needing those. Thank goodness we got the rejoicing gear in yesterday. Hey, come on, start practising. Everybody get ready. There'll be a huge rush. People will go berserk with joy.

(Everyone waits, keyed up with anticipation, but no one enters. After a time, CUSTOMER 1 stamps in and goes to the festival counter.)

Customer 1:   Here! Take your rotten festival junk back again. I want a refund.

Religious festivals: *(Stunned.)* We don't give refunds.

Customer 1:   In that case, I'll talk to my solicitor. Your stuff never worked. Where's the Wailing Department?

(CUSTOMER 1 goes over to wailing area, WAILER 1 moves to greet him or her and they talk quietly. CUSTOMER 2 enters angrily and goes to the songs section. There is obvious amazement and consternation among shop staff.)

Customer 2:   Aghh! So much for your songs. Didn't tell me that wasn't what the Lord wanted, did you?

Religious songs: What?

Customer 2:   Take your song and shove it up your nose! The Lord is really angry with me for robbing the old girl. Do you have wailing here?

Religious songs: Yes, over there.

(CUSTOMER 2 moves to wailing area as CUSTOMER 3 enters.)

Customer 3:   I'm suing you lot! That sacrifice was about as much use as an ice works at the South Pole. Wailing is what I need.

Grain offerings: Over there.

(CUSTOMER 3 moves to wailing area. Phone on wailing desk rings.)

Wailer 1:   Yes, this is the wailing section. *(To WAILER 2.)* Quick, get over there and deal with the people at the counter.

Wailer 2:   I'm sorry. We weren't planning for a big demand for wailers. We're the only two available. If you just wait outside, we'll get to you one at a time.

(CUSTOMERS exit angrily.)

Wailer 1:   *(On the phone.)* Sorry, but we're fresh out of wailers. You'll just have to wait till we get more in. *(Hangs up.)* Where are we going to get more wailers ?

Wailer 2:   There are a few apprentices out the back. But they've only done half of the required six week course.

Manager: *(Rushing on.)* What's going on?

Wailer 1:   Everyone wants wailing, sir.

(Phone rings again. WAILER 2 answers it and speaks briefly, then hangs up.)

Wailer 2:   More requests for wailers, sir.

Manager: How many?

Wailer 2:   Four.

Manager: *(To the other ASSISTANTS.)* Quick, you lot. Get with it!

All: But we don't know how to wail.

Manager: Then you're fired!

All: Wahhhhh!

Manager: That's fine. All you have to do is get out and do that. Now practise before you go.

(They move to side to practise. Phone rings again.)

Wailer 2:   Hello. What's that? That's awful. Okay. I'll tell him. *(Hangs up.)*

Wailer 1:   What is it?

Wailer 2:   There's a national wailer shortage. The day of the Lord is here. It's a disaster. Chaos! People are being punished for not looking after the poor and needy.

Manager: What? But what about all the songs, festivals, offerings, sacrifices? All given to the Lord?

Wailer 2: Apparently that's not what the Lord wanted.

Manager: But what did the Lord want?

Wailer 2: Justice, caring, honesty, relief of poverty.

Manager: Well who would have thought of that!

Wailer 2: Not only that. Unqualified wailers are being used to fill the gaps.

Wailer 1: What?

Manager: Shocking.

Wailer 2: Out in the country, farmers are stepping in and doing some part time wailing.

Wailer 1: We studied for years to become wailers, and now this lot of amateurs comes in, just to make money!

Assistants: Hey. We think we got it. How's this. Wahhhhh!

Wailer 1: Don't get smart, you lot. You got a long way to go yet.

Wailer 1: I'm not having unqualified staff doing our job. This is a matter of demarcating. Call the Union!

All: The Union!!

Union rep: Hello. I represent the Greenpieces organisation and we're running a campaign to save the wailers.

Manager: Oh, forget that. This whole place is in chaos! You mob. Get out there and start wailing.

(The ASSISTANTS and UNION REP race out wailing as they go.)

You, *(Pointing to WAILER 1.)* start ringing round to see if there are any retired wailers who want some extra income. *(To WAILER 2.)* You see if this rejoicing equipment can be converted to wailing standard. Oh, this is all a mess. Now we find out the Lord wanted justice, caring and honesty. If only we'd listened to Amos! The day of the Lord wasn't what we'd expected it to be!

(Blackout on generally chaotic and panic-stricken scene.)

© 1992 THE JOINT BOARD OF CHRISTIAN EDUCATION
Noah and the Tubes: 15 short plays for churches
by Chris Chapman, Susan Chapman, Peter Gregory and Heather Allison

QUESTIONS FOR DISCUSSION

The group should first familiarise itself with conditions in Israel in the mid-8th century B.C. Especially note that it was a time of apparent prosperity and religious piety. Note also the way Amos, in his role as prophet, was able to see through this to the injustice beneath it. The concept of 'The Day of the Lord' should also be examined (Amos 5:18).

1. Quickly scan Amos 1:3-5 and 2:1-3. What reaction would this preaching receive in Israel? Why?

2. Read Amos 2:6-16. What reaction would this receive in Israel? Why?

3. Scan chapters 4 and 5, and list 6 crimes for which punishment will come.

4. See Amos 5:21-24 and 6:5. What similarities are there between this sort of religion and an insurance policy? Compare James 1:26-27.

5. What do you think, in Amos' view, would constitute true religion?

NO DEPOSIT NO RETURN

There are actually two playlets here. They may be performed separately or together.

CHARACTERS

George   Frances   Mildred   Irving

SCENE	*Shows four characters sitting and standing round in suitably formal postures in a garden party setting. George is absorbed in a newspaper.*
Mildred:	George.
George:	Humph!
Mildred:	I say, George.
George:	Humph!
Mildred:	Don't humph, George. It doesn't become you.
George:	No, my angel.
Mildred:	George, do you see what I see?
George:	Yes, my angel. Anything you say.
Mildred:	Good, because I thought I was dreaming.
George:	Fine, dear.
Frances:	Mildred, dear. I say, there's something happening on the croquet lawn.
Mildred:	Yes, George said he saw. Didn't you, dear?
George:	Yes, my little rose petal.
Mildred:	See?
Irving:	I don't really think they should be there, do you, Frances?
Frances:	No, Irving, definitely not. A very disturbing sight indeed, Irving. Not really the sort of chaps we like around here.
Irving:	Mildred dear, tell George that we don't think those are the sort of things that should happen on one's croquet lawn. After all, the neighbours will gossip.
Mildred:	George, dear. Sorry to disturb you again, but Irving, Frances and I have just been talking and we really don't think that 5,000 people congregating on the croquet lawn is quite the done thing. What do you think?
George:	No, my little flower of the desert.
Mildred:	Oh dear. They've trampled the azaleas.
George:	*(Slamming down his paper.)* What? Good grief! What's happened to the azaleas, and what are all those people doing on the croquet lawn?
Mildred:	Looks as though they're about to have lunch, George.

George: Then why wasn't I told we were having guests?

Frances: We didn't invite them.

George: Well, who did then?

Irving: Perhaps it was the little bearded man in the long white smoking jacket.

George: (*Calling.*) I say. Chap! Excuse me, chap. Couldn't you feed your 5,000 somewhere else? They're upsetting the hounds.

Mildred: I don't think he can hear you, George. There's too much talking.

George: Bother! This is all such a bore. Look, Irving, be a good fellow, would you, and take this twenty cent donation for food expenses over to the fellow in the white gown and say that this is probably a very worthy cause and all a very nice show, but we can't have chappies tramping round the lawns. And make sure you get a receipt.

Irving: Oh, bother! Now I'll have to use my legs. Couldn't Gerrard carry me?

Frances: Oh, Irving. Don't be such a wimp!

(*IRVING exits looking somewhat pained.*)

George: This is a real pest! Why can't they hold their rallies somewhere else?

Mildred: My goodness. They're going to start eating.

Frances: No, it's alright. They've only got some bread and fish. Must be afternoon tea for the speakers.

Mildred: They'd better not leave a mess in the garden, though.

George: Hang about. The leader is breaking up the bread and fish and handing it round to everyone. What does he think he's doing? Performing a miracle?

Mildred: In our garden too!

Frances: What will the neighbours think?

Irving: (*Returning.*) What an odd chap he is. I handed him the twenty cents but he said he didn't need it and that his father would provide sufficient food from the little they had. He said that those people had followed him for many miles and that he must feed them.

Mildred: Well, everyone's eating now.

George: And look at the mess they're making.

Frances: About twelve basket's full, I'd say.

Irving: What is the world coming to? It's the thin end of the wedge, I tell you! Once you treat people like them as equals, they'll want to go to heaven just like us! And it's not on, I tell you!

(*Lights quickly fade as the rest agree solemnly. Lights are brought up quickly again if you are doing these two playlets together.*)

(*The same four are standing and strolling, looking round them, obviously in some fairly impressive building.*)

Irving: Wonderful church you have here, George.

George: (*Modestly.*) It's not my church.

Irving: May as well be. You paid for most of the things in it.

Mildred: George is so considerate.

Frances: You certainly are, George. There's no doubt about it.

Mildred: Oh my goodness.

Irving: What is it, Mildred?

Frances: Yes, Mildred. Do tell.

Mildred: Look!

All: (*Looking in the direction indicated.*) Gasp!

George: (*Quite fascinated.*) It's a poor person. How novel.

Irving: How do you spell that, George?

George: P.o.u... p.o.e.r... p.o.o... Wait. Look. She's going to put in a donation.

Mildred: I can't quite see how much.

Irving: I can! It was a few five cent pieces.

George: Oh, dear. How paltry!

Irving: I haven't seen those for years.

Mildred: What's a cent?

Frances: Money, I think.

Mildred: Is that like gold?

George: A little bit. But gold buys a lot more things.

Frances: (*Jumping up and down.*) Oh goody. Can I buy something?

Irving: Who does she think she is anyway? Putting in such an embarrassing amount. Why doesn't she just go away? I'm sure God isn't interested in her five cent pieces.

(*They start to move offstage.*)

Mildred: Throw another gold bar in the collection, George.

George: Do you think we should? After all, we do have to pay for the house in Bermuda.

Mildred: Good thinking. Let's not throw money away.

Frances: Perhaps we could throw in half a bar next week.

Irving: Every little bit helps.

George: At least we don't embarrass God by throwing in a few cents, eh, chaps? What fine fellows we are.

(*Solemnly and smugly agreeing, they process offstage. Blackout.*)

QUESTIONS FOR DISCUSSION

1. See Mark 12:41-44. Compare it to Luke 18:9-14. What is similar in each of these stories?

2. Think of an example where information about a person's background could completely change the way you view their actions.

3. Think of a situation where you or someone else has jumped to a conclusion about someone else, and has then had to back off.

4. Why was the widow's offering worth more in real terms?

5. See 1 Samuel 16:7. How does this verse relate to the lesson seen in the story of the widow's offering?

SCHOOL'S IN

(Episode One)

CHARACTERS

Jesus	Ian Incredibly-Rich
Mary Magdalene	Ethel Ethereal
James	Phil Pharisee
John	Sid Scribe
Peter	Miss Interpret

SCENE: *The stage is set up as a school classroom. Kids enter to some appropriate musical piece to do with school, for example 'To Sir With Love'. PETER is dragging his net. MISS INTERPRET enters the classroom.*

Miss Interpret: Alright, you kids! Sit down and be quiet or I'll have to do something unfortunate!

(She fires a pistol into the air. There is complete and sudden silence from the class. They stand, all except PETER who is still shocked into a dream.)

That's much better. Stand up please, Peter.

Peter: Sorry Miss.

(A quarrel over something breaks out between PHIL PHARISEE and SID SCRIBE.)

Miss Interpret: Those two up the back , would you please...

Peter: *(Turns on the two)* Yeah, shut up for miss or I'll...

Miss Interpret: No, Peter!!

(PETER drives them into the floor with both fists in a tremendous hammer blow.)

Peter: Next time I'll cut your ears off. I've done it once and I'll do it again!

Miss Interpret: Thank you, Peter, but that wasn't necessary.

Peter: Sorry, Miss.

Miss Interpret: Now can we have some order? Good morning, 10B5.

Class: Good morning, Miss Interpret.

Miss Interpret: Be seated. Now just keep a little quiet, please, while I call the roll.

James and John: Here, Miss.

Miss Interpret: James and John, but I haven't called you yet.

John: But mum said we have to be first on the roll.

James: And I'm going to be the first out of us two.

John: Are not!!

(They begin to fight.)

Miss Interpret: Alright, alright! Hmmm. The two brothers.

Both: Here miss.

Miss Interpret: Mary Magdalene.

Mary Magdalene: Here miss. Rock on. *(Giggle.)*

Miss Interpret: Phillip Pharisee.

Phil: Yeah, and my name should be in front of Mary Maggott over there.

Miss Interpret: Sidney Scribe.

Sid: Yes, Miss.

Miss Interpret: Next is...

Ethel: *(Gasp.)* I see it in the cards, the future! My name is about to be called !

Miss Interpret: Ethel Ethereal.

Ethel: You see. The cards never lie. Here, Miss, physically. Spiritually, I am elsewhere.

Phil: Wish ya were somewhere else. Why don't ya go bend a spoon, ya witch?

Miss Interpret: Ian Incredibly-Rich.

Ian: Here, Miss, in style. The golden carburettor on the Daimler broke down and Eric had to drive me in the Jag. It's so slow.

Miss Interpret: Peter of Galilee... *(no response)*... Peter of Galilee... Rock!

   (PETER jumps over, knocks over a desk and laughs dumbly.)

Class: *(General cheering.)* Good on you, Rocky.

   (They break into some suitable tune or well known movie theme while Peter raises his fists high and grins happily round at everyone. Amid the mayhem, MISS INTERPRET again reasserts her control.)

Miss Interpret: Quiet please! Now, today I have a very sad announcement.

Class: Awwwww!

Miss Interpret: The school board has decided that the curriculum we have been teaching you for the past 1500 years is to be modified with a new teaching method and content. Therefore, you are to have a new teacher.

Class: *(Pause to look at each other. Then, all cheer except PHIL and SID.)* Whoopee!!

Phil: You mean you're not teaching us any more, Miss?

Miss Interpret: No, I will be taking another class.

Sid: But, Miss, Phil and me are top of the class in the old method.

Miss Interpret: Well, you'll just have to get used to the new method.

Phil: But Sidney Scribe and me know all the laws.

Sid: And we can recite them all.

Phil: Backwards.

Sid:	And we don't see why we should put up with this new method. As a matter of fact...
Both:	*(They break into some suitable protest song such as 'We're Not Gonna Take It', thumping lustily on the desks. PETER stands and raises a chair or desk above his head to hit them.)*
Miss Interpret:	No, Peter, no!
	(PHIL AND SID see their danger and duck beneath the desk. PETER turns smilingly to the teacher for approval or instruction, desk still raised above head.)
Miss Interpret:	*(Soothingly)* Just put the desk down, Peter.
	(PETER obeys slowly.)
	Now class, I trust you'll listen to the new teacher as well as you've listened to me. Maybe even a bit better. Good morning, 10B5.
Class:	*(Rises)* Good morning, Miss Interpret.
Ethel:	*(Jumping to her feet and gasping.)* Look, the cards show that we are about to get a new teacher!
	(JESUS enters.)
Ethel:	You see! The cards never lie.
Jesus:	Good morning, 10B5. I'm your new teacher, Mr Jesus. You can call me Mr Jesus or Sir. Let's get out our books, we have a lot of work to do. Now let's get started on the first of our new ideas. My father designed the new curriculum and method and it all revolves round one single person. That person is the key to everything.
Phil:	Who's the person!
Jesus:	You'll find that out as we go.
Sid:	*(Leaping up.)* Don't know, do you? Huh? Huh? Huh?
Jesus:	Do you know?
Sid:	Nup!
Jesus:	Then you'd better sit down and be quiet.
Sid:	*(Sits.)* Awww!
Jesus:	Now, it's nearly recess time.
	(Class cheers and breaks into some song which expresses an escape idea such as 'We Gotta Get Out of This Place', or breaks into an excited rabble.)
Jesus:	Quiet, please. The bell hasn't gone yet. After recess, I will give you some special one to one teaching and we'll work through some problems together.
Phil:	You'll get a bit of one to one from Mary Maggott, sir.
Sid:	Yeah, Mary Maggott. We know what you do after school.
Mary:	I do not. Just because I...
Phil:	You got maggot germs.

Mary:	Well, have some then!
	(She reaches out and touches one of the two who immediately shrieks and wipes the 'germs' onto the other. A tussle occurs which is quietened by JESUS as the others laugh.)
Jesus:	Quiet up there!!
Phil:	Well, just keep her away from us.
Jesus:	As I was saying, the lessons in the new method will be specifically designed for each person's individual needs and ability.
Ian:	You'd better give Peter a book with pictures. He can't read.
Peter:	Why you...
Jesus:	Sit down, Peter.
Peter:	Sorry, Sir.
Jesus:	Now, during recess, I want you to think about the ideas I'm going to give you. When we come back in, you can tell me what impression they made on you. Maybe you'll get a new angle on life. Maybe you'll get a clue about the identity of the person this whole course revolves round.
Sid:	I still reckon he doesn't know.
Jesus:	Mary, here's yours.
	(MARY stands.)
	You are stained red with sin. I will wash you as white as snow. Though your sins are deep red, you will be white as wool.
	(MARY accepts the thought, ponders for second and then exits.)
	James and John, here is a thought for you. Whoever wants to be first must place himself last and be the servant of all.
James:	I'll be the first to find out what it means.
John:	You will not. I will be.
	(They exit fighting.)
Jesus:	Phil Pharisee and Sid Scribe.
	(They both stand)
	I and the Father are one.
Phil:	*(Gasp!)* I'll tell my dad about this!
Jesus:	Where is your dad?
Phil:	He's down looking after the shop. *(SID viciously stamps on his toe.)* Umm, I mean the temple.
Jesus:	I'll have to have a talk to him some day.
	(PHIL and SID exit muttering.)
Jesus:	Ian Incredibly-Rich.
	(IAN stands.)

Go and sell all your possessions and give the money to the poor.

Ian: Well, I'll have to think about it. But there is polo practice, and the yacht club...

(He exits muttering also.)

Jesus: Peter. Peter. Rock!!!

(There is a general smashing as Peter wakes up and stands clumsily.)

I assure you, if you have faith the size of a mustard seed...

Peter: I haven't got a face the size of a mustard seed.

Jesus: No, no, Peter. Listen. If you have faith the size of a mustard seed, you can say to this hill, 'Go from here to there' and it will go.

(PETER stands smiling blankly at JESUS.)

Er, you can go now.

(PETER gathers us his net.)

What's that you have?

Peter: *(Proudly)* A net.

Jesus: Why did you bring a net to school?

Peter: Well, mum made me fish sandwiches for lunch, and I meant to take them but the net smells like fish and I got confused and took it by mistake. Then again mum smells like fish too, like lots of things around our place.

Jesus: Why don't you just eat the net?

Peter: Hey, what a great idea.

(He goes off with his net but it has become entangled round the leg of a desk and he takes the desk with him until JESUS disentangles him. PETER is smilingly embarrassed and grateful and exits.)

Ethel: *(The noise brings her out of her trance.)* Oh! Oh! Smashing furniture. Poltergeist! Poltergeist!

Jesus: Ethel, settle down. Your thought is, 'No man comes to the father but by me'. And if you want an extra clue look up Deuteronomy 18 where it says, 'Don't let your people practise divination or look for omens or use spells or charms, and don't let them consult the spirits of the dead'.

Ethel: Hmmm. I'll have to check out what the tarot cards say on that one.

Jesus: I wonder how they'll go with these new ideas.

(Glances at watch.)

I'd better get down to the tuck shop before it closes.

(JESUS exits as the lights fade to blackout.)

SCHOOL'S IN

(Episode Two)

(KIDS return as bell rings or similar suitable sound effect is heard.)

Jesus: Now, how did you all go with all the things I said to you? Did you think about them? Hey, where is Ian Incredibly-Rich?

John: He ran away down the road.

James: Even the Daimler couldn't catch him.

John: He kept saying something about not being able to give up the yacht club.

Jesus: Oh dear. I was afraid it might affect him like that.

Ethel: I foresaw it all in the Ouija board. I knew he'd run away.

Jesus: And you, Ethel. Did you get anything out of what I said to you. No one comes to the Father but by me?

Ethel: Well, I had a terrible time. First I checked the crystal ball and the tarot cards, and then I danced beneath the moon. I spun the bottle, and threw it over my left shoulder but it broke and now I've got seven years bad luck. And I cut my toe on the fragments. While I was running to the bathroom for a bandaid, I went under a ladder and kicked a black cat. I tried looking in that verse from Deuteronomy but it wasn't specific enough so I'm blowed if I know what you mean. Well, I've got to go now. Remember, if you want your palms read, I'm the one to see. I'm good at reading palms, but you'll have to provide a ladder if they're over two metres high. May the powers be with you all.

(ETHEL sweeps out.)

Jesus: Well, I can see she got a lot out of that! James and John, how did you go?

(Silence.)

James: You first.

John: No, you first.

Jesus: Enough said. I see you got the message. Mary Magdalene, how about you? What did you make of 'you are stained red with sin. I will wash you clean as snow'.

Mary: I thought about it a lot. I've got another chance. That meant a lot to me. Thank you.

Jesus: How about you, Peter? What did you get out of my message about faith?

Peter: I need to rely on God more and stop trying to handle it all my own way.

Jesus: Did anyone find out the person whom this all revolves round?

Peter: *(Excitedly.)* Yes, Sir. I did. It's you!

Jesus: You've got it, Peter.

Phil: Right! That's it! I've had enough!

Sid: I've had enough too. We discussed your blasphemous little claim to god-head.

Phil: And I'm going right down to the shop...

(SID stamps his foot.)

I mean the temple, and telling my dad.

Sid: Me too.

Jesus: Boys, your dads aren't in the temple right now. You see, during recess, I went down and had a little talk to them myself.

Phil: Oh yeah?

Jesus: Yes. Your dad was quite reasonable. We had a great chat, as I was over-turning his tables. And your dad will be out dry-cleaning his robes. One of the sacrificial animals stood on him on its way down the temple steps.

Sid: *(Gasp)* You'll pay for this!

Jesus: Yes. I know.

Peter: Wherever you go, I will go, Master.

Jesus: Who is coming with me?

James John, Mary, Peter: We are!

Phil and Sid: Not us.

(The latter two settle into singing some protest song such as 'We Don't Need No Education' and the others exit happily together as lights fade to blackout.)

*Peter attends school
for the first time
(And wonders "Why?")*

QUESTIONS FOR DISCUSSION

Read the specific verses given in the play as lessons.

> Deuteronomy 18:9-13
> Matthew 17:20
> Mark 10:35-45
> John 14:6
> John 3:16-17
> John 10:30
> Isaiah 1:18
> Matthew 19:16-23

1. Which one of these lessons do you think applies personally to you? Why?

2. Are there other Bible verses through which you have felt God teaching or speaking to you?

3. Explain the reaction of the Pharisee and Sadducee to the idea of a new system. What was the old system in which they were so skilled? See Matthew 5:17-20 and then examine the teachings of Jesus in Matthew 5:21-24, 31-32, 33-37, 38-42, 43-48.

4. In each of the above readings, how is Jesus expanding and improving on the old system?

5. See John 2:13-22 for another reason Jesus became unpopular with the religious leaders.

THE JEREMIAH STORY

CHARACTERS

Jeremiah	Prophet 3
King	Shemiah the high priest
Prophet 1	Edward the butler
Prophet 2	

Narrator on stage who becomes singer of final song
Voice over (preferably some well-known voice of minister, youth leader or someone else in authority whose voice will be recognised by the audience)
Assorted party guests and Babylonian soldiers who may actually be members of the band which plays to accompany the song at the end.

SCENE: *The humour of this drama partly depends on the dreadfully formal and posh dress and body language of the party guests who are never in the least bit flustered at the sight and sound of Jeremiah's sufferings. Only at the end do they seem somewhat discomforted. It also depends on the ability of Jeremiah to bounce back like a piece of rubber no matter what the treatment he receives. It is good if you can arrange for him to pop up in a different entrance each time, getting zanier as the play progresses. Have him coming down through the audience, in windows, up through the floor or down from the roof. Anything you can come up with.*

It is also good if the NARRATOR does his whole introductory talk visible on stage with JEREMIAH and the false prophets, PROPHETS 1, 2, 3 on stage with him covered with sheets. This way he can unveil them as he introduces the audience to them.

Narrator: Hello, children. Well, today we have an exciting story of one of the great prophets of the Old Testament. Do you know what prophets are? That's right. They're what daddy's business doesn't make any of. But this is a different type of prophet. It's a special person with a special message from God. The prophet we hear about today is called Jeremiah. He was the youngest of the prophets, but despite that fact, he did some great prophet type work.

Jeremiah lived in the far away land of Judah. Of course, if you lived *in* Judah it wasn't a far off land, but from our point of view...

Voice over: Come on, keep going.

Narrator: Sorry. The people of Judah were very bad. Lots of false prophets *(unveil the false prophets on stage)* were telling the king the wrong thing and God decided to send Jeremiah to tell them to clean up their act or they'd all be up the creek. Not that up the creek is any worse than down the creek. I suppose it all depends on...

Voice over: *(More exasperated)* Hurry up!

Narrator: *(Obviously realising that his job is at risk more and more.)* Now Jeremiah was very young when God called him. *(Unveils Jeremiah who is dressed in a nappy and drops onto all fours.)* God sent him a special message. *(A rolled up piece of paper is thrown onto the stage from off, or above or anywhere unseen. It lands in front of Jeremiah who picks it up and reads it.)* And Jeremiah took it straight to the right place. *(Jeremiah stands and visibly grows older as he reads till he is striding off the stage majestically.)* Of course, the responsibility made him grow up very quickly on the way.

Voice over: *(Exasperated groan.)* Get on with it!

Narrator: *(Flinches.)* You can imagine the scene at the royal garden party at the house of Shemiah, the high priest.

(As NARRATOR speaks, the scene forms up onstage. Guests, high priest enter and take nonchalant positions chatting silently and sociably.)

All the high society of Judah would have been there, all the prophets, priests and big wigs.

(NARRATOR exits quietly.)

Edward: *(Announcing.)* His Majesty, King of Judah, Lion of Jerusalem, Defender of the Temple.

(KING enters and Shemiah runs over to kow tow. Applause from all guests as KING enters.)

King: Thank you, my subjects. Shemiah, as high priest, you should have a few reputable prophets round whom you could recommend.

SHEMIAH: Most assuredly, your majesty.

(He runs about rounding up the three prophets who gather with abnormally cheesy grins and ingratiating body postures before the KING.)

Shemiah: Here are the three finest prophets in the land, your majesty.

King: Their names?

Shemiah: Er, Prophet One, Prophet Two and Prophet Three.

King: *(Obviously unimpressed.)* Yes. Well, gentlemen, pray inform me as to the state of the nation.

Prophet 1: My Lord, prosperity shines on you with the light of a thousand suns. You are the finest, most astute king we have ever had.

(General polite applause and favourable comments from crowd as PROPHET 1 completes his or her little tribute and bows obsequiously.)

Prophet 2: Noble sire, wisdom smiles from you with the light of the moon and stars. You are the wisest king since Solomon.

(Crowd applauds again.)

Prophet 3: Oh noble one, your riches sparkle like the camp fires of the bedouin tribesmen. You are the wealthiest king in the universe.

(General crowd applause, etc. Note that it is almost impossible to overplay these three prophets. They are obviously crawlers of the worst sort and are keen to outdo each other in buttering up the king. Their movements can reflect this and may become more ridiculous as the play goes on to the point where they are kissing shoes, shining cuff links, brushing coats, etc. as they speak.)

Jeremiah: *(From the background, offstage or in the audience.)* No he's not. He's a twit!

All: *(Swing round to see who spoke.)* Gasp!!

Jeremiah: *(Rushing onstage.)* Like I said, he's a twit. And so are all of you with that nonsense you're saying! You're not from God. None of you are, you mob of crawlers! *(Puff, pant.)*

Shemiah: Pardon, majesty. This is Jeremiah. He's not sane. He doesn't know what he's saying, the young fool. I don't know how he got in or even what he's doing here.

Jeremiah: I'll tell you what I'm doing here. I'm here to tell you that God sent me a vision. I have seen a giant pot, boiling and seething away in the north. And it's going to spill over in this direction!

Shemiah: Must be the bolognaise boiling over. Excuse me. *(Races off.)*

Jeremiah: No, it's not the bolognaise. It's the enemy from the north. They're coming and they'll wipe you all out if you don't stop this idolatry and sinning that's going on. The Lord has told me !

Prophet 1: *(Soothingly.)* Pay no attention to this man, majesty. He is not sound.

Prophet 2: Besides, he is a mere youth with no experience in prophecy.

Prophet 3: What does he know? What he speaks of will never come to pass.

Jeremiah: It will too! Your whole country will be broken in pieces like, like this pot.

(He grabs a pot from the tray of a passing waiter and smashes it on the floor just as SHEMIAH returns from the kitchen.)

Shemiah: *(Gasp.)* My genuine, pre-Exodus, antique Egyptian jar... ruined! Edward!

Edward: Yes, sir?

Shemiah: Have this fellow removed, beaten and thrown in chains.

Edward: Certainly, sir. Which chains shall I use, sir?

Shemiah: The ones mentioned in the book of Jeremiah, chapter 20.

Edward: Certainly, sir. *(Grabs JEREMIAH roughly.)* Come along, young man. It's time for your nap.

Jeremiah: *(As he is being dragged out.)* Don't say I didn't tell you. It's coming. You'll all be...

(The party guests smilingly watch him dragged off. Once JEREMIAH is offstage, they quietly listen, heads raised a little. Through the PA come the most horrible grinding groans, clanking of chains, weights, heavy metal gates, etc. Once the sounds stop, the guests laugh nonchalantly to each other and continue their quiet chit chat as though nothing had happened.)

King:	Now where were we? Oh, yes. Prophets, some comment on the people.
Prophet 1:	Majesty, your people look to you with love and loyalty burning in their hearts.
	(Applause, etc. from the crowd.)
Prophet 2:	Sire, the temple is daily filled with worshippers. Prayers go up by the thousands. The people praise the Lord who sends us these messages.
	(Crowd applause.)
Prophet 3:	My Lord, your people are as a shining light of goodness among the heathen. Their moral example casts out shining rays like a glowing fire in...
Jeremiah:	*(Struggling in from somewhere, loaded with chains.)* No, it doesn't. They're a mob of cheats, swindlers, slave drivers and rogues. They worship idols, bully the weak and profane the Lord's name. And if you, kingo, don't do something about it and clean this place up, you'll have armies marching through here and all the people of this city will be killed or taken away into exile!! *(puff, pant.)*
Shemiah:	*(Claps his hands twice.)* Edward. The underground cell.
Edward:	The one mentioned in Jeremiah, chapter 38, sir?
Shemiah:	Precisely.
Edward:	I've already had it prepared, sir.
Shemiah:	*(Confidentially.)* Oh and Edward. See that he falls down the steps, would you?
Edward:	With pleasure, sir.
	(Again, Jeremiah is seized and dragged off shouting.)
Jeremiah:	Don't listen to these cheap B grade prophets. They don't come from God! They don't...
	(Again the guests are impassive at this spectacle and again they listen. Over the PA comes the sound of a door opening, a kick landing on something soft and a series of bumps, ouches and ows fading, suggesting someone theatrically being kicked down a long flight of steps.)
King:	Young idiot. He's really becoming quite disturbing. Still, I suppose we must expect immaturity from one so young. Now, gentlemen. What of the future?
Prophet 1:	Majesty, the future shines upon you as bright as burnished gold.
	(Applause.)
Prophet 2:	My Lord, you are the sun of all our tomorrows.
	(Applause.)
Prophet 3:	Sire, peace and prosperity are ever our companions on the road of life.
	(Applause.)

Jeremiah:	*(Crawling out of some ridiculous entry point.)* Rubbish! It's going to be death, doom and destruction unless something is done to clean up the morals of this place. And further more...
Shemiah:	Edward.
Jeremiah:	Turn back to the Lord, all of you, or else...
Edward:	The well, sir?
Shemiah:	The one mentioned in Jeremiah, chapter 38.
Edward:	The one with the mud in the bottom. *(Grabs JEREMIAH.)* Come along, young man. It's time for a little swim.
Jeremiah:	*(Being dragged off again.)* The king will be captured along with all the rest. You'll be led away in...
	(They listen for the sounds again. There is a long fading scream followed by a distant but recognisable raspberry or similar sound that indicates JEREMIAH has hit the mud in a big way. Crowd goes on chatting and laughing again. There is a knock at the door.)
Shemiah:	Edward, see who that is, would you?
Edward:	*(Briefly goes and returns.)* It's the Babylonian army, sir.
King:	What was that, Edward?
Edward:	The Babylonian army is at the gate, sire.
King:	Probably collecting for *(insert name of well known local charity or similar cause)*. Give them fifty cents.
Edward:	Sire, they've already taken the entire treasury.
King and Shemiah:	What?
King:	What a dashed cheek.
Edward:	The whole city's full of them, sire.
King:	What? Why wasn't I informed we were having guests?
Edward:	They're not guests, sire. They've taken over. Something like Jeremiah said they would.
King:	What?? Prophets! Explain this! You said you had a word from the Lord.
	(The PROPHETS and the party guests have been looking increasingly perturbed by all this. Now, the PROPHETS race forward and fling themselves nervously at the KING'S feet. They form some ridiculous posture such as all joining hands or all placing their hands on the head of PROPHET 1.)
Prophet 1:	Er, um, I foresee... I foresee...
Prophet 2:	An important phone call. For me.
Prophet 3:	And me.
Prophet 1:	Me too.
	(They quickly race out.)

King:	Call the army.
Edward:	What army, sire?
King:	Er, Edward, call me a taxi.
Edward:	Very well, sire. You are a taxi.
King:	Fool! How am I supposed to get out of this city?
Edward:	May I suggest as a prisoner of war, sire?

(*With that dreadful announcement, the drum beat for a rap song strikes up live or on tape. Babylonian soldiers in uniform invade the stage and stand in two groups downstage left and right. King, party guests and Shemiah recede to upstage centre. Jeremiah comes on and joins them together with the false prophets, so they can all take part in the dance which accompanies the song which is essentially a retelling of the story. As each party is mentioned in the story, they can jump forward and jive round. The singer, who is actually the NARRATOR from the start in suitable costume for the song, now races onstage and begins his routine.*)

Narrator:
Jeremiah, Jeremiah
Was a stubborn little trier.
God would send his message via
Him just like a telephone wire.
Take it, Babylonians...

Babylonians: (*In apelike grunts.*) Ooh! Ooh! Telephone wire. Ooh! Ooh!

Narrator:
Jeremiah, Jeremiah
Told them to repent or die-ah,
Told the king now listen, sire,
Your city's headed for the fire.
Take it, Babylonians...

Babylonians: Ooh! Ooh! Fire and smoke. Ooh! Ooh!

Narrator:
Jeremiah, Jeremiah
Up against the royal liars.
Prophets all were up for hire,
Sold out to the richest buyer.
Take it, Babylonians...

Babylonians: Ooh! Ooh! Richest buyer. Ooh! Ooh!
Now we're here, they didn't listen
To the man who tried to tell them
That the Lord would punish all their dirty tricks!
Ooh!
When the Lord sends warnings to ya,
Then you'd better listen careful,
Otherwise you'll end up in a nasty fix.
Ooh!

Narrator:
Jeremiah, Jeremiah
Didn't give up or retire,
Told them what the Lord required,

His words were an electrifier.
Take it, Babylonians...

Babylonians: Ooh! Ooh! Electrifier. Ooh! Ooh!

Narrator: Jeremiah, Jeremiah
Speaks to us here in 'Austraria',
Says the situation's dire,
Needs to be a rectifier.
Take it, Babylonians...

Babylonians: Ooh! Ooh! Rectifier. Ooh! Ooh!
When you think you got it worked out,
And you think that God can butt out,
That's when you are running on a risky chance.
Ooh!
Don't think you can do without God,
He's the one who runs the system,
Calls the shots and wrote the music for the dance.
Ooh!

Narrator: Read the book of Jeremiah,
Learn the lesson, walk the wire,
Make God's will your heart's desire,
Let your aim be ever higher.
Take it, Babylonians...

Babylonians: Ooh! Ooh! Ever higher. Ooh!

Narrator: Take it, Babylonians...

Babylonians: Ooh! Ooh! Jeremiah. Ooh! Ooh!

(During the last chorus and refrains, the BABYLONIANS have chained or tied the KING, PARTY GUESTS, SHEMIAH, FALSE PROPHETS, etc. into a long line and now singing the refrain for as long as is necessary, they conga line offstage as prisoners of war and the lights go down to blackout.)

QUESTIONS FOR DISCUSSION

Before commencing these questions, the group needs to be aware of the background of political events surrounding the fall of Samaria in 721 B.C. and of Jerusalem in 587 B.C. Information can be found in 2 Kings 22-25 and 2 Chronicles 34-36. It is also recommended that some understanding is gained of the religious and political role of the prophet in the Old Testament, especially as a moral conscience, social critic and interpreter of God's plan in current political and social processes.

Jeremiah provides a good example for us because his times were similar to ours today, being characterised by confusion, insecurity, crumbling values and political instability.

1. Jeremiah 1:4-10. What purpose did Jeremiah believe that God had for him?

2. Why was Jeremiah's task so difficult? See Jeremiah 16:9; 4:19; 17:16.

3. Despite his sense of Gods calling, Jeremiah experienced inner conflict. How is this seen in the following verses? Why do you think it occurred? Jeremiah 12:1; 15:10 and 15:18.

4. Old Testament prophets frequently used dramatic symbols and Jeremiah was no exception. Look at these examples and find out what Jeremiah was explaining. Why did he do it this way, and not simply tell them? Jeremiah 19 and 27.

5. Jeremiah was not the only prophet around. What motives do you think animated prophets like Hananiah? (Jeremiah 28 and 23:11-40)

6. What criticism did Jeremiah have to make about current religious practices? See Jeremiah 7:9-12; 8:8-10 and 19:14-15.

7. For 23 years, Jeremiah called for repentance. Why do you think the people of the day refused to listen to warnings such as that given in Jeremiah 25:8-11? Are there lessons in this for us?

8. For details of some of the trials Jeremiah went through, see Jeremiah 18:18, 20:1-2, and chapters 37 and 38. Why do you think Jeremiah continued to speak out? What can we learn from him?

9. Are there prophets today? Who are they? Do people heed their warnings? Why or why not?

10. See Jeremiah 7:9-11 again. What would Jeremiah have to say about organised religion as opposed to personal religion? Can the two ever be the same?

THE HILLBILLIES

CHARACTERS

Ma	Elly May
Pa	Jethro
Grandma	Jesus Boy
Grandpa	Smith Boy

SCENE: *Slides of country scenes come up on screens placed to either side of the stage. Centre stage light comes up to reveal a family of hillbillies sitting on the ground or chairs and relaxing. Their opening words can be combined into a song or simple rhythm if so desired.*

Ma: I'm a country Ma.

Pa: I'm a country Pa.

Grandma: I'm a country Grandma.

Grandpa: I'm a country Grandpa.

Elly May: I'm a country girl.

Jethro: *(Silence. They all look at JETHRO, but he is daydreaming. PA hits him on the head with a hat.)* I'm a country boy. Sorry, Pa.

All: Yeah, we is country folks.

Pa: How many chillun' we got this year, Ma?

Ma: Well, let's see. There's John Boy, Mary Ellen, Jim Boy, Jim Boot, Elly May, Billy Sue, John Junior, Little John, Friar Tuck-In, Jimbo Joe John, Boy John, Jim Jams and John John.

Pa: Gee, we nearly got a John in every room.

Elly May: Sure is a beautiful day in this here Galilee country side, Pa.

Pa: Yep, sure is a beautiful day, Elly May.

Ma: What's on today, Pa?

Pa: I'm gonna take young Jethro here and fix them fences, repair the tank, chip the beans, pick the tomatoes and feed the hogs... *(Thinks a bit.)* Well, maybe tomorrow.

Ma: I like a man who's not afraid of work.

Grandma: *(Without prompting.)* I had a cat once.

Grandpa: No, you didn't.

Grandma: Good, I hate cats.

Jethro: Sure is quiet in this here Nazareth town.

Elly May: Yep, nothin' ever happens in this here town of Nazareth, ever since the feud finished.

Pa:	Yep, we sure showed them Samaritans.
Ma:	Samaritans and us never did get on.
Jethro:	How come, Pa?
Pa:	It goes back a long way, Jethro.
Elly May	Who's that down there in the lower paddock, Pa?
Ma:	*(Pulls out a gun.)* Is it a Samaritan?
Pa:	*(Pulls out a pair of binoculars.)* Nope.
Ma:	Darn, I suppose I could shoot them anyway.
Pa:	Easy, Ma, feudin' time is over. We is livin' in peace and harmony now.
Ma:	*(Puts gun away.)* Sounds boring to me.
Jethro:	*(Looking through the binoculars.)* Hey, Pa, you know that big bull in the lower paddock?
Pa:	Yep.
Jethro:	I think there's something wrong with it.
Pa:	Why?
Jethro:	It's pregnant.
Elly May:	Wonder if it'll be a boy or a girl.
Ma:	It'll be a calf, Elly May, don't you know nuthin'?
Grandma:	That sun is sure hot.
Grandpa:	Well, don't touch it.
Grandma:	Sure is quiet 'round this place.
Ma:	Been quiet ever since Mary and Joseph Davidson lost their eldest.
Jethro:	Yep, sure was sad. Was the best horse I ever did see.
Ma:	Not the horse! The son! The Davidson's oldest boy – Jesus. Pa, hit that boy!
Pa:	*(Goes to hit JETHRO but can't reach.)* I can't reach. Jethro, bring your head over here. *(JETHRO does so and PA hits him with a hat.)* Thanks, Jethro.
Jethro:	No worries, Pa.
Grandpa:	Yep, sure is quiet since Jesus Davidson left Nazareth. He always was a strange boy. Never did amount to much.
Grandma:	He was a smart aleck kid. You remember that time they all went to the big city for the Passover and he stayed behind in the temple to talk all them book learnin' types?
Ma:	Yeh, givin' cheek to grown ups.
Pa:	I heared he done tried a bit of farmin' with pigs. I heared they all upped and ran down to the water and drowned.
Ma:	They probably saw Jethro comin'. *(They all laugh.)*

Jethro:	And I heared he's been takin' up doctorin' and healing people that have got lameness, withered hands, death and stuff like that there.
Elly May:	And I heared he done taken up with a bunch of fishermen and weirdos. They go wanderin' the countryside without jobs, or work or nuthin'.
Ma:	Lazy bums.
Jethro:	I heared he's done got into music.
All:	Music!!
Jethro:	Yeh. 'Cause it says in Mark chapter three that he got together a band of twelve men.
Ma:	Pa, hit that boy.
Pa:	Jethro... *(JETHRO bends towards PA so he can be hit. Pa hits him.)* Well, this here Jesus Davidson is doin' all these things and turnin' water into moonshine. I heared about it from that weddin' shin-dig. I reckon he's gettin' tickets on his self and is tellin' people he is somethin' special.

Jethro:	Look, Pa, there's someone a comin'.	*(These lines need to be*
Pa:	Look, Ma, there's someone a comin'.	*passed round fairly*
Ma:	Look, Elly May, there's someone a comin'.	*excitedly and rapidly.)*
Elly May:	Look, Grandma, there's someone a comin'.	
Grandma:	Look, Grandpa, there's someone a comin'.	
Grandpa:	Look, Jethro, there's someone a comin'.	

Jethro:	Hey, yeah!!
Elly May:	He looks like one of them Smith boys.
Ma:	Which one?
Elly May:	I dunno, just one of them.
Pa:	Sure are a dumb family them Smiths.
Smith boy:	Hi, I'm one of the Smith Boys.
Pa:	Which one?
Smith boy:	I dunno. Just one of them.
Pa:	Sure are a dumb family them Smiths.
Smith boy:	Anyways, my Pa, he says to give you Kettles a message.
Grandma:	Well, what's the message?
Smith boy:	He's comin'.
Grandpa:	Who's comin'?
Smith boy:	He.
Pa:	Sure are a dumb family, them Smiths.
Smith boy:	You insultin' my family?
Pa:	No, *I'm* insultin' *your* family.

Smith boy:	That's alright then.
Pa:	Sure are a dumb family, them Smiths.
Grandpa:	He must mean the Davidson boy.
Grandma:	Yep, that's it, Jesus Boy Davidson must be comin' home.
Smith boy:	Yep, that's it, that's the message. Well, I gotta be gettin' home cause Ma's a cookin' up a mess of vittles. *(Hesitates.)* Er... which way was my place? *(Family all point in different directions. SMITH BOY nods happily and runs out through audience, tripping over as he goes.)*
Ma:	Well, what do you think of that? Jesus Boy Davidson's comin' home.
Elly May:	Well, I'll be hornswaggled.
Ma:	Well, I'll be a cross-eyed needle threader.
Pa:	Well, I'll be a three legged pole vaulter.
Jethro:	Well, I'll be. *(They all look at him.)* That's it. I'll be.
Grandma and Grandpa:	Pa, hit that boy.
Pa:	Jethro. *(PA hits JETHRO as per routine.)*
Grandma:	He'd better not come around here putting on his fancy airs, and makin' like he's something special. He might be able to fool them city types but not us.
Grandpa:	Yeah. We knowed him since he was no higher than a snake's belly in a wagon rut.
Elly May:	Yeah. I know his sisters.
Jethro:	Yeah. And I know his brothers.
Elly May:	Hey, Pa.
Pa:	Yeah?
Elly May:	Jesus Boy is comin' down the road.
	(JESUS BOY enters.)
Jesus Boy:	Hey, you all. Hey, Ma and Pa Kettle. Grandma and Grandpa Kettle. Hi, Elly May and Jethro Kettle. Long time since I seen you folks.
Jethro:	That's because it's a long time since you left.
Pa:	Be quiet, Jethro.
Jesus Boy:	How's your liver been all this time, Grandpa?
Grandpa:	Oh, not so bad. Comin' along alright. Soon be ready to put back in.
Elly May:	Did ya hear we got television?
Jesus Boy:	Yeah! Is it any good?
Ma:	Be better when we get electricity.
Jesus Boy:	Speakin' of power, I've got great news for you folks.
Ma:	Here we go.

Jesus Boy: The kingdom of God is comin' real soon, so you all gotta start lovin' each other and your fellow human beings.

Pa: Seems I heard that repentance bit before.

Grandpa: Yeah, John Boy the Baptist was always on about that.

Grandma: An' look what happened to him.

Ma: Yeah, he ended up with his head on a plate.

Elly May: Yuk, what a way to go.

Jethro: Yeah, imagine bein' on a plate with all them vittles up your nose and in your eyes and stuff.

Ma: Pa!!

Pa: I'm sick of hittin' him. Jethro hit ya self. *(JETHRO hits himself.)*

Jesus Boy: What I was talkin' about is that we gotta love each other and start obeyin' God's commandments. Like, turnin' the other cheek and stuff like that.

Grandpa: Turn the other cheek, eh? Good idea.

Grandma: Yeah, Jethro, maybe you could hit ya self on the other side. Ha, ha, ha.

Jesus Boy: *(Obviously frustrated.)* That's not what I meant. I didn't want to make fun of Jethro. What I'm tryin' to say to you folks is that me and the father are one. Anyone who has seen me has seen the father.

Elly May: Yeah, you always did look like ya dad down the road.

Jesus Boy: No, not my earthly father, my heavenly father. I am the way, the truth and the life. No one comes to the father but by me.

Ma: You mean to tell us you is some kinda prophet?

Pa: Ha, ha. He's havin' a little joke with us, Ma. We all know his Ma and Pa is just the folks down the road.

Jethro: Yeah, once a carpenter's son, always a carpenter's son.

Pa: That's very profound, Jethro.

Jesus Boy: No, I'm telling you now, I was sent to show you what God is like.

Grandma: Oh, come on now, Jesus Boy, don't push a good thing too far.

Grandpa: We's know'd you since you was in nappies.

Elly May: Hey, if you is God, why don't you do somethin'?

Grandma: Yeah, I got a bad headache. Why don't you fix it, Jesus Boy. *(JESUS BOY places his hand on GRANDMA's head and then stands back.)*

Pa: Well, Grandma, how do you feel?

Grandma: Well, I do believe I feel a lot better.

Ma: The headache was probably going to go anyway. Grandma is pretty healthy.

Pa: Yeah, it was probably that spring tonic she was drinkin' this mornin'.

Jethro: You mean that stuff she gets from the little boiler in the hills? The one with the curly pipe goin' into it? *(PA digs him in the ribs so he'll be quiet.)*

Ma: Why don't you do somethin' really big?

Pa: Why don't you make it rain on the bottom paddock?

Elly May: Why don't you clear them saplings from the hillside?

Grandma: Why don't you make Jethro think?

(All family members burst into laughter.)

Jesus Boy: Well, do any of you folks think I can do those things?

All: Nope!!

Jesus Boy: Well, how do you expect me to do anything if you got no faith in me? That's what miracles work on, you know - faith.

Pa: We don't have no faith in you, boy, 'cause we know that you is just one of us local yokels from Nazareth Hollow.

Ma: Yeah, you're a nice kid but you sure got tickets on you self.

Jesus Boy: I kinda knew it was gunna be like this. Prophets is never accepted in their own home town. See ya 'round, folks. *(JESUS BOY exits.)*

Pa: Sure is quiet around here.

Grandpa: Fancy that Jesus Boy Davidson reckonin' he is some kinda prophet.

Ma Yep, this Galilee Country just ain't prophet country. *(They all nod and agree.)*

(Lights fade on the group mumbling to each other and the curtains close.)

QUESTIONS FOR DISCUSSION

Matthew 13:53-58
See also Luke 4:16-30

1. What risk did God take in coming to earth in the form of a human?

2. What advantages for us were there in God's coming to earth in the form of a human?

3. Did Jesus experience human life in every way just as we do?
    Matthew 4:1-11
    John 4:5-7
    Mark 4:38
    John 11:35
    Luke 22:39-44
    John 21:9-13

4. Do you think Jesus had a sense of humour?
    Luke 9:51-54 and Mark 3:16-17 (to be read in conjunction)
    Matthew 19:24
    Matthew 14:16
    Matthew 7:3

5. Why did locals have more trouble accepting Jesus as someone special than people away from the home town did?